Rooms Colors Dreams

Amy England

American Letters & Commentary, Inc.

Rooms Colors Dreams

ISBN-10: 0-9825647-2-4
ISBN-13:978-0-9825647-2-1

Published by
American Letters & Commentary, Inc.
PO Box # 830365
San Antonio, TX 78283

www.amletters.org

American Letters & Commentary, Inc., is a not-for-profit corporation under section 501(c)(3) of the United States Internal Revenue Code. For over twenty years, AL&C has been dedicated to publishing innovative and "difficult" writing. We are immensely grateful to both the English Department and to The College of Liberal and Fine Arts at The University of Texas at San Antonio for their generous support of our journal. The views expressed in this book, however, are not necessarily those of UTSA, its administration, its employees, or its students, nor are they necessarily the views of AL&C's editors, its volunteers, or its donors.

Cover Design/Book Layout: David Ray Vance

Rooms Colors Dreams

Amy England

Acknowledgments:
Gratitude for the use of conversations with Brianna Douglass, Lucinda England, Owain Guinn, Mary Olson, Matthew Michael, Veronique Perrot, Robert Uptain, and others.

Dedication:

You Know Who You Are

ROOM	COLOR	DREAM
An Empty Room	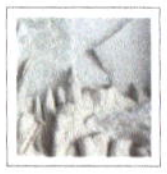	A Dream of Invisible Ink
The Haunted Wallpaper	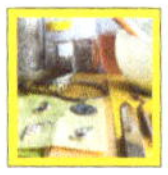	A Dream of Violence
Jane Eyre's Alcove	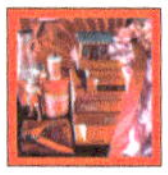	The Red Theater
The Lobby of the Sky Hotel	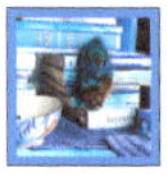	The Alchemical Key
A Dark Chamber	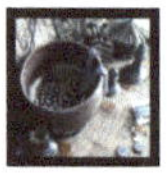	The Dream of a New Currency
The Beautiful Melancholy of Cardboard	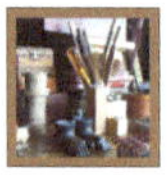	Clove Tea
A Decayed House	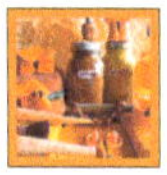	The Male Championship
The Caged Garden	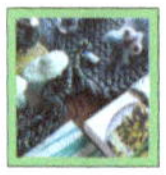	Operatic Cucumber
Alien Laundry Room	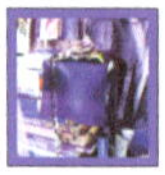	This Is How I Sleep
Interrogating Children	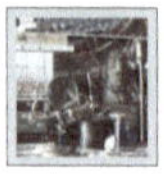	Movies with My Uncle

ANIMAL	VEGETABLE	MINERAL
A White Rabbit. No Whale	Virgin Plants	Bleach. Salt. Snow
Come Closer Yellow Animal	A Sunflower Clock. Daffodils of Death	Yellow Ochre. Yellow Gold. Yellowcake
A Creature Defined by Its Insides	Fugitive Madder Lake	Vermilion and Mercury Poisoning
Blue Foot Fetish	Indigo Interview	From the Stadium of Crayons
The Black Amphibians of Mt. Roraima	Black Cooking Smells	Iron Ink
The Elaborating Serpent	Death by Opium Cake	To the Dark Tower Came
Animals who Are on Fire	The Tiger Crop	Ruby Sulfur
The Flying Turtles of Honan	The Grass Hour	Testing the Poison Plate
Frankenstein's Nudibranch	Many Toxic Purple Flowers	The Drunken Amethyst
Not a Unicorn	Good Fungus. Bad Fungus	Circular Metals

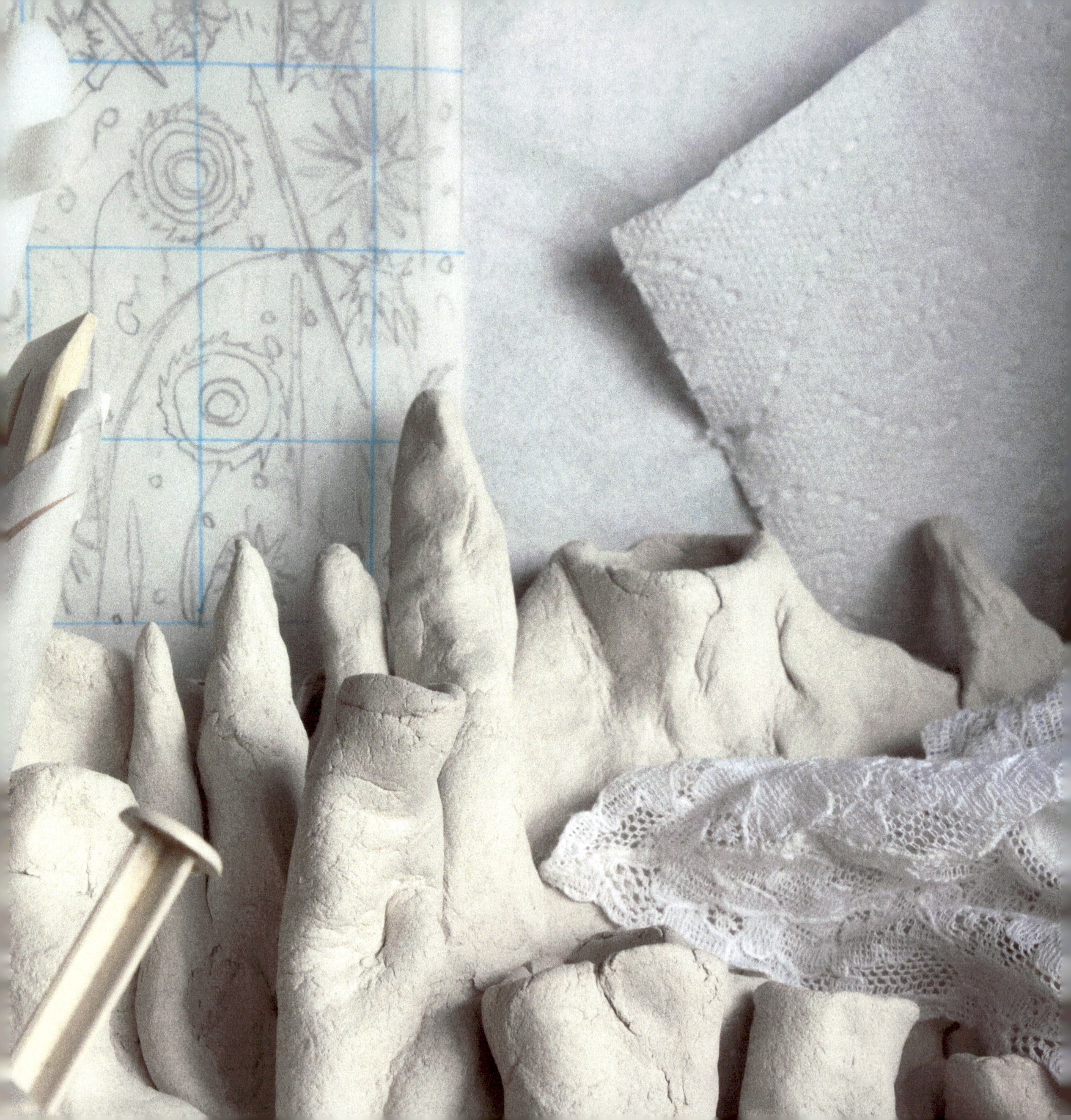

AN EMPTY ROOM

To each color its vessel. And here, rendered in coffee stirrers and popsicle sticks, is the first vessel I can remember. My mother took me to see our new house. I understood that we were going to live here, but I thought we would live in it like this, empty of furniture, and I thought that was the best idea I'd ever heard of…I was about two and a half. Those white shoes that toddlers wear were in the lower periphery of my vision as I sat on the floor, clapping. My mother clapped along, and I assumed, no division of self and world, that we were in agreement about the furniture.

I have a number of questions I like to ask people. For example, when does the world feel the most real? At first I expected them to answer with some variation on a moment of stillness, but people have said things like, when I'm engaged in strenuous physical activity, when I'm exerting my will against resistant circumstances, when I'm suffering, when I'm ill.

I have two experiences that inform this particular question. One of them is walking out on the first really cold morning of winter, a bright white winter day, and hearing the rustling of sparrows in the bushes. The cold makes the sounds distinct, and I'm suddenly aware of the whole world of animals and plants going on with their secret lives away from my sight.

The other is even simpler: sitting in a room, looking up from reading, and the light falls through the window. Maybe that is because light falling through a window is my first memory. Another favorite question: what was your first powerful aesthetic experience? Again, the answers are not what I expect, and often involve scale: a whale, a grove of redwoods. And again I started with several examples, and am not sure which came first, but probably this was the first one. The white room full of New Mexico sunlight, the freedom to move with nothing in the way. The white light and the breeze pouring through the window as if they were the same thing.

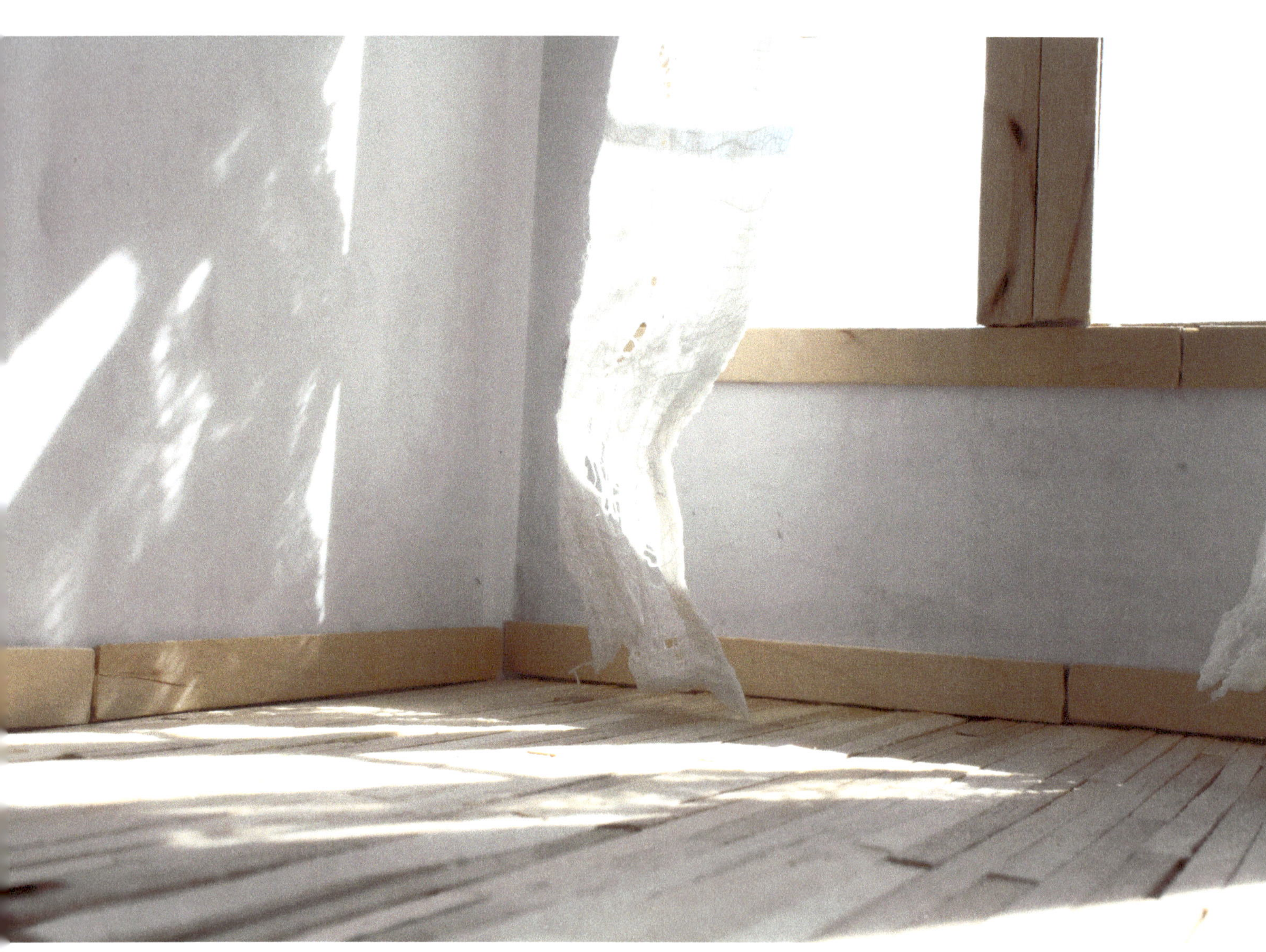

In Germany, the 17th century Jesuit monk and polymath Athanasius Kircher examined a version of the camera obscura, and provided an illustration in one of his books. The print shows a square chamber erected out of doors, and within that another chamber made of paper. The outer walls have pinholes through which the sunlight can project the scene outside upside down onto one of the inner paper walls. A person enters the inner chamber through an opening in the floor to watch the projection. Kircher claimed "that he could even see the teeth of the men standing outside."[1]

The first stage of eye development is just a patch of photoreceptor cells. They can distinguish light from the dark, but not shape, direction, or color. If it benefits the animal, gradually a chamber evolves, concave or convex, so that the angle of light entering the chamber can provide more information, like the direction of sun or moon, of prey or predator. Then a glassy membrane forms over the chamber to protect it. Eyes are two rooms into which light falls.

WHITE EMPTIES OUT

Kircher also claimed to have invented (but perhaps only improved upon) the MAGIC LANTERN, the ancestor of the slide projector and the movie projector. Consider what images people chose for these first projections. One of Kircher's illustrations shows the lamp casting through the painted slide and onto the wall the image of Death as a skeleton, with his scythe: the magic lantern in its infancy already deserved its other name, the phantasmagoria.[2]

Kastan: "The 'innermost idea of this hue' is that it doesn't have an innermost idea. White becomes our symbol of symbols precisely because of this vacancy."[3] Wilkie Collins repeated this symbol of symbols with an almost insane insistence. In *The Woman in White,* Anne Catherick appears suddenly in the night to Walter Hartright, disappears just as suddenly, and haunts him afterwards. When he first sees Laura Fairlie, her fairness and faintness and strong resemblance to the woman in white make her seem like a ghost of a ghost. The two repeat each other throughout a novel full of white notes, *starred with flashes*, culminating in Laura, supposedly dead, taking the place in the asylum of the other woman, actually dead, so that when her friends go to see Anne, they find Laura, "the dead-alive," in her place.

□

White looks at you in accusation: Are you pure? Are you innocent? Are your sins washed away? Is your kitchen fully sterilized? Or are you full of conflicting wants? Needlessly complicated? Extraneous? Messy? White's demands are those of an unbroken egg, austere to the point of impossibility.[4] *How happy to the eye—the true white of my beloved's fan.*[5] No division between self and other. Yosa Buson often wrote of white as the purity of undivided desire. The source for this idea winds back to the Chinese classic *Huai-nan Tzu:* "Yang-tzu saw a forked road and grieved that it would branch south and north. Mo-tzu saw raw silk and wept at the thought that some would be dyed yellow and some black."[6]

Clear fair pale blank blanched bleached. Kenya Hara writes about white as an emptying out, so that there is room for the imagination to engage, for an exchange to occur. A few sketched ink lines on a Japanese folding screen direct us to imagine white as a snowy mountain, or trees covered by fog. White is also the lingering of remnants. Ghosts and bones.

> According to one of the most prominent experts of kanji ideograms, Shirakawa Shizuka (1910-2006), the Chinese character for white (白) was modeled after the shape of the human skull. This is supposedly because the image of white held by the people who lived back then was based on the sight of abandoned skulls in the fields, bleached by wind, rain and sunlight. Obviously, such unexpected encounters must have left their mark. The traces of life contained in the color white strikes us when we come upon animal bones in the desert, or shells along the seashore.[7]

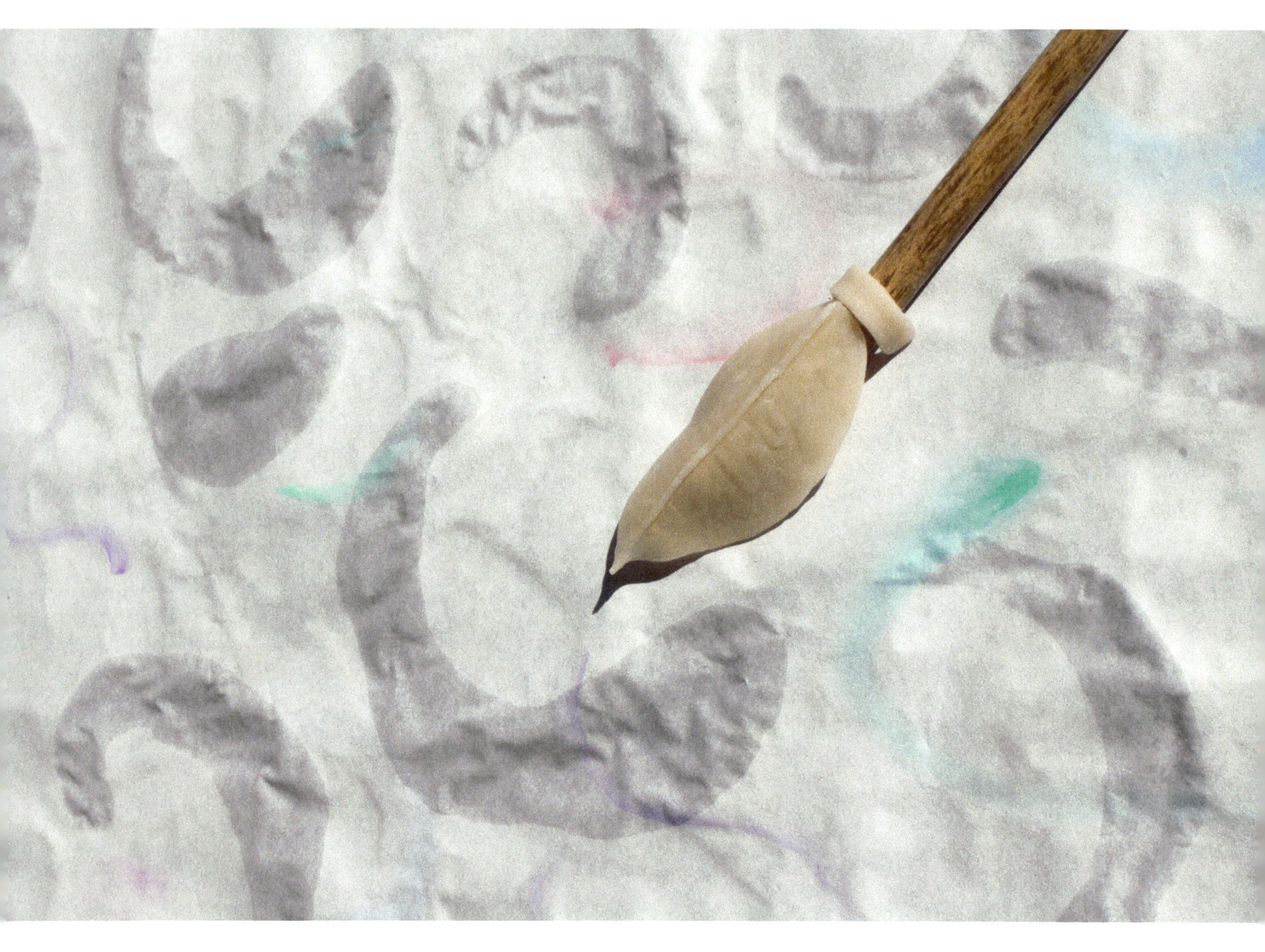

A DREAM OF INVISIBLE INK

A lot of aged academics now 'have rooms' in my old college dormitory, as if my college has become Oxford in 1920 (which it has not). I meet with one of these venerable beings and follow her, at her invitation, into her study. All the while she is unwrapping a new set of brushes. They have tips of various sizes of some soft flexible translucent white material that look like folded lotus leaves. In response to my fascination, she shows me how to use them on the paper set up on the easel. One wants to make extravagant flourishes with the weird tips but that is not in keeping with the discipline, and anyway the long straight correct strokes do produce wonderful wavy accidents. We dip the pens in water and oil, not wanting to waste ink on mere exercises, and make barely visible marks on the white paper, faint traces of color appearing in the strokes. So that the paper almost remains empty. Each color a realm, with its own laws and treasures. It is hard from here to bear that the threads will be dyed. It is hard to leave this room.

□

White light. How it behaves. Very occasionally we can see from the pier, with the moon at a certain angle and the waves of Lake Michigan rising a certain way—many and low, not long and high—that the water will focus the light in the oddest way. The moonlight becomes pure solid white, snaking through curved letters of an alien alphabet over and over. In no way does it seem a product of the uneven surface of the water: the light trails look as if they were above or below it, and sometimes give the uncanny sensation that we can see through a thin spot in this world into another.

A WHITE RABBIT AND NO WHALE

The way to the Secret lay through the mystery, hitherto impenetrable to all of us, of the woman in white: On the train last summer, there was this woman. She had an unwieldy pile of books and a notebook balanced on her lap, and she had the top book open, writing notes in the margins. Her hair matched her exquisitely crisp bleached linen shirt. Her handwriting was spiky and old-fashioned and almost readable from where I sat. I spied on her shamelessly and tried to make out the titles of her books. We left the train, and she exited before us, walking ahead of us wherever we went, our own personal white rabbit. I wanted to talk to her and be her and read exactly what she was reading. When we got to the outdoor concert where our friend was playing the flute, she was sitting before us in the audience. One of the books she carried was Mark Smith's *From Sight to Light,* which says that Plato thought the colors were all derived from black and white.

□

But the empty room might not be my first memory. Recently, my mother asked me, do you remember that poem I taught you? *Serene the silver fishes glide, stern, pale lipped, and wonder-eyed*—you were only eighteen months old; you could hardly pronounce it. And I realized that I had carried around all that time not the words, but a picture, like a child's drawing, of silver fish with wide white eyes swimming in black water. Which tells me about how my mind works. It might even tell me something about how children see things—maybe their drawings are actually quite true to their perceptions. And how memory works: The first time I consciously remembered the image of the fish, I thought, it looks a little like a Klee painting, and now I see something much closer to a Klee painting than my original image. In fact, now I can't recover the first image at all; I can only remember remembering it.

Here is the poem from which I have inaccurately quoted the first lines:

At the Aquarium

Serene the silver fishes glide,
Stern-lipped, and pale, and wonder-eyed!
As through the aged deeps of ocean,
They glide with wan and wavy motion.
They have no pathway where they go,
They flow like water to and fro,
They watch with never-winking eyes,
They watch with staring, cold surprise,
The level people in the air,
The people peering, peering there:
Who wander also to and fro,
And know not why or where they go,
Yet have a wonder in their eyes,
Sometimes a pale and cold surprise.

To each color its action. White: I see. Let's start there, with the whites of the eyes, which show where someone is looking, and the degree of their astonishment.

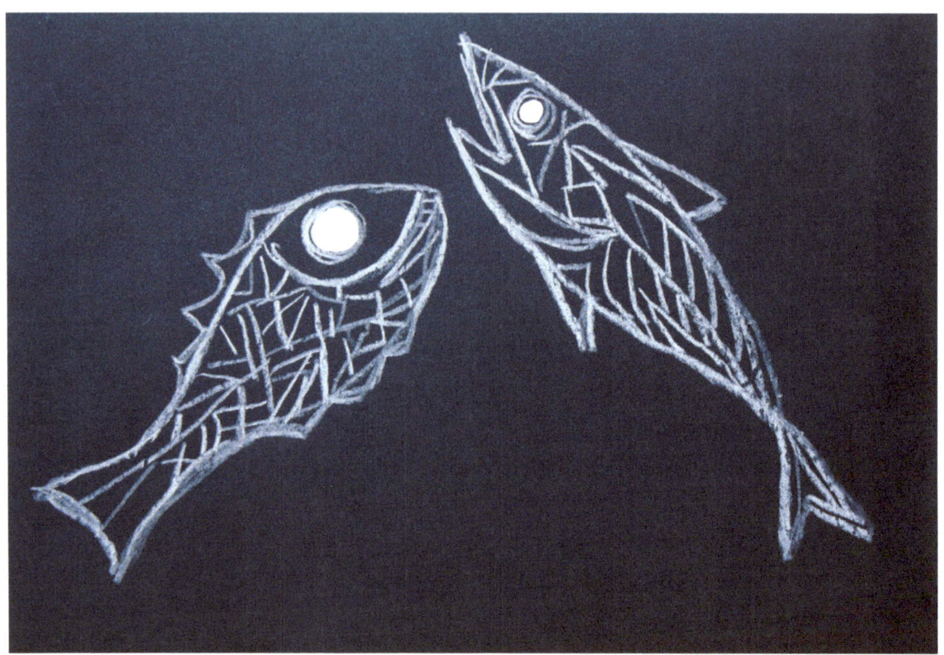

The aquarium is apt also. *The blowfish shows to the world above the whites of his eyes...*[8] We are mostly going to stay inside. Batchelor discusses admirably the whited sepulchres of Conrad's outreaches of empire, the whiteness of the whale, but we are not going to do this.[9] There is plenty of empire to be seen indoors. Here, to take a page (literally) (sort of) from *Tristram Shandy,* is the page where the whale is not:

VIRGIN PLANTS

I have written before about an encounter with a lily. I was sliding down a muddy wooded hillside trying to reach the train home. I caught myself on a tree and there it was, perfectly white and all alone in the forest, staring at me.

My grandmother said that when she was a girl (in that far away Iowa paradise, where Queen Victoria never died), she was given a vanilla milkshake to drink before bed because she was so thin and delicate. Everyone said I was like a white lily, she said. Every night she took the glass in her delicate hand out of obedience rather than appetite, and reluctantly raised it with her thin, graceful wrist. When she put her own daughter, my mother, to bed, she poured into her drowsy ear this poisonous myth of virginal purity. She used to read her, for example, "The Lady of Shallott," who wore *a crown of cloudwhite pearl,* who was *all raimented in snowy white.* And since my grandmother was the matriarchal beginning of all literature, those two things, literature and virginal purity, came into being yoked together.

Am I a white lily, Mama? asked my mother, a small child. A tiger lily maybe, said my grandmother.

Raiment of linen bleached with

BLEACH SALT SNOW

sodium hypochlorite. An emptying out. Swimming pool burn in the nose and the color flees. Swallowing the negation of color can cause "gagging, pain and irritation in the mouth and throat; pain and possible burns in the esophagus and stomach; vomiting; and shock can appear right away to within a few hours."[10] Finally, the white clothes I had always longed for, and then a truck drove by and spattered me all over with mud. White leads also to that heartbreak.

Lead based white paint is wondrous, going on smoothly and evenly and lasting for decades, but then the sweet tasting chips find their way into children's mouths…Finlay also talks about Victorian women poisoning themselves to lighten their skin with lead-based cosmetics. She even says that in the first stages, the symptoms must have made the women think, with satisfaction, that they were turning into the Lady of Shallott, "'dead pale,' but with 'a lovely face.'"[11]

An ice cube and a glass jar of salt. Is color light or matter? Here is purity: the sunlight passes through the just cleaned window and sets its rhomboid down on the polished floor, as if no glass were there at all. But

Newton took a prism and found all the colors folded into white light, like the sticks of a fan. Goethe asked scientists to sign an oath never to so heretically unfold the light again.

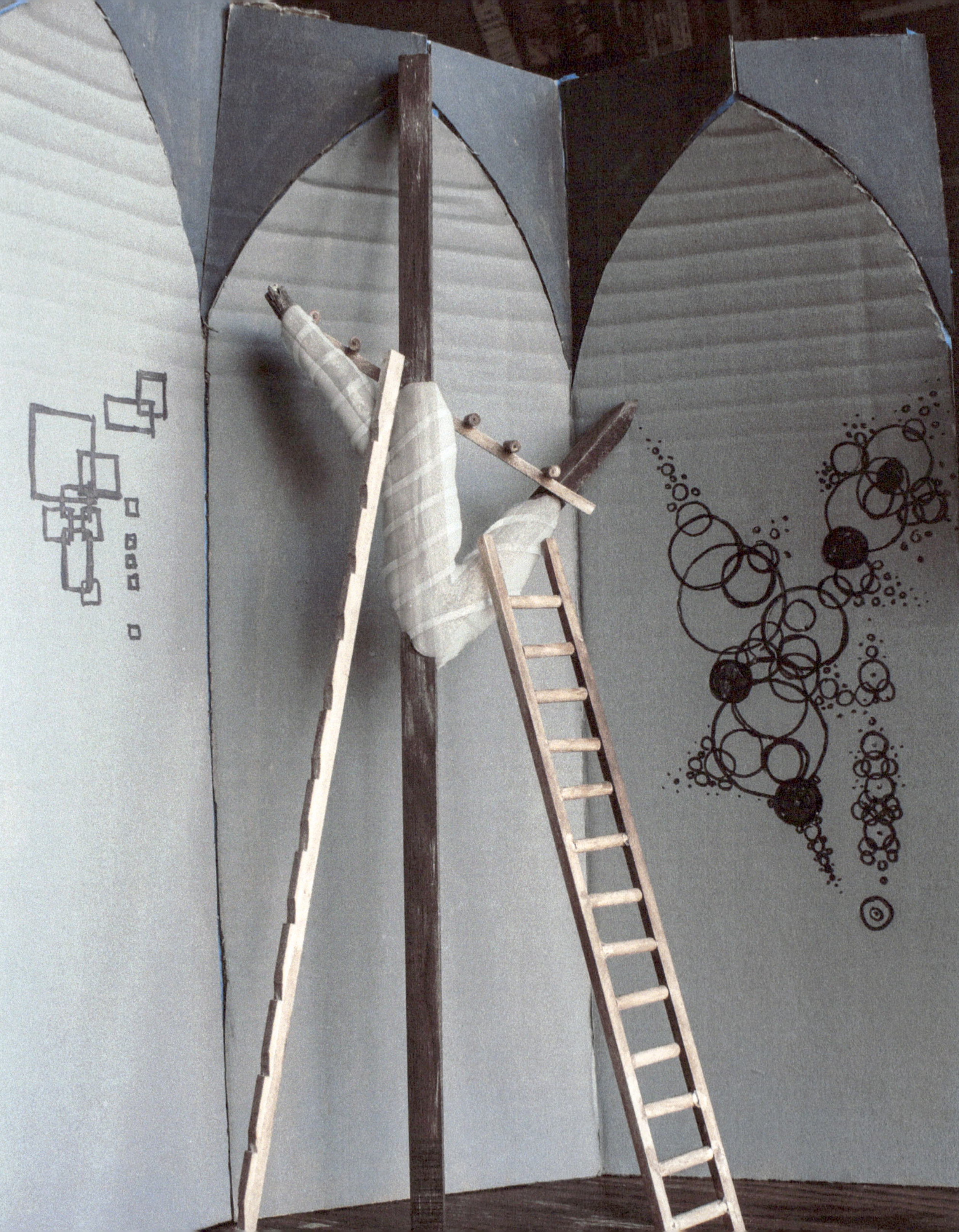

We push open the door to the observatory and enter to find, not a telescope, but a large resonant crystal. It has accreted around the wooden struts and central pillar like glass honeycomb. It has internal white diagonal stripes. One branch of it follows a simple pattern of black squares, while the other translates that design into a delicate web of ink fractals on the wall. I see all the ladders that surround the crystal (it is being *worked on*) and ask permission to climb up and study it more closely. The docent agrees, and I pull off the sheet of cardboard that covers the first ladder. As I climb, many small obstacles have to be pushed aside, and I'm not a third of the way up before the ladders get too small and flimsy to continue.

In the far corner of the room, in the far corner of the folding screen, the mountain side is covered with snow, and the mineral ozone smell of snow, indistinguishable from the dry of the cold. And the snow throws all its ice needle colors right in your eyes.

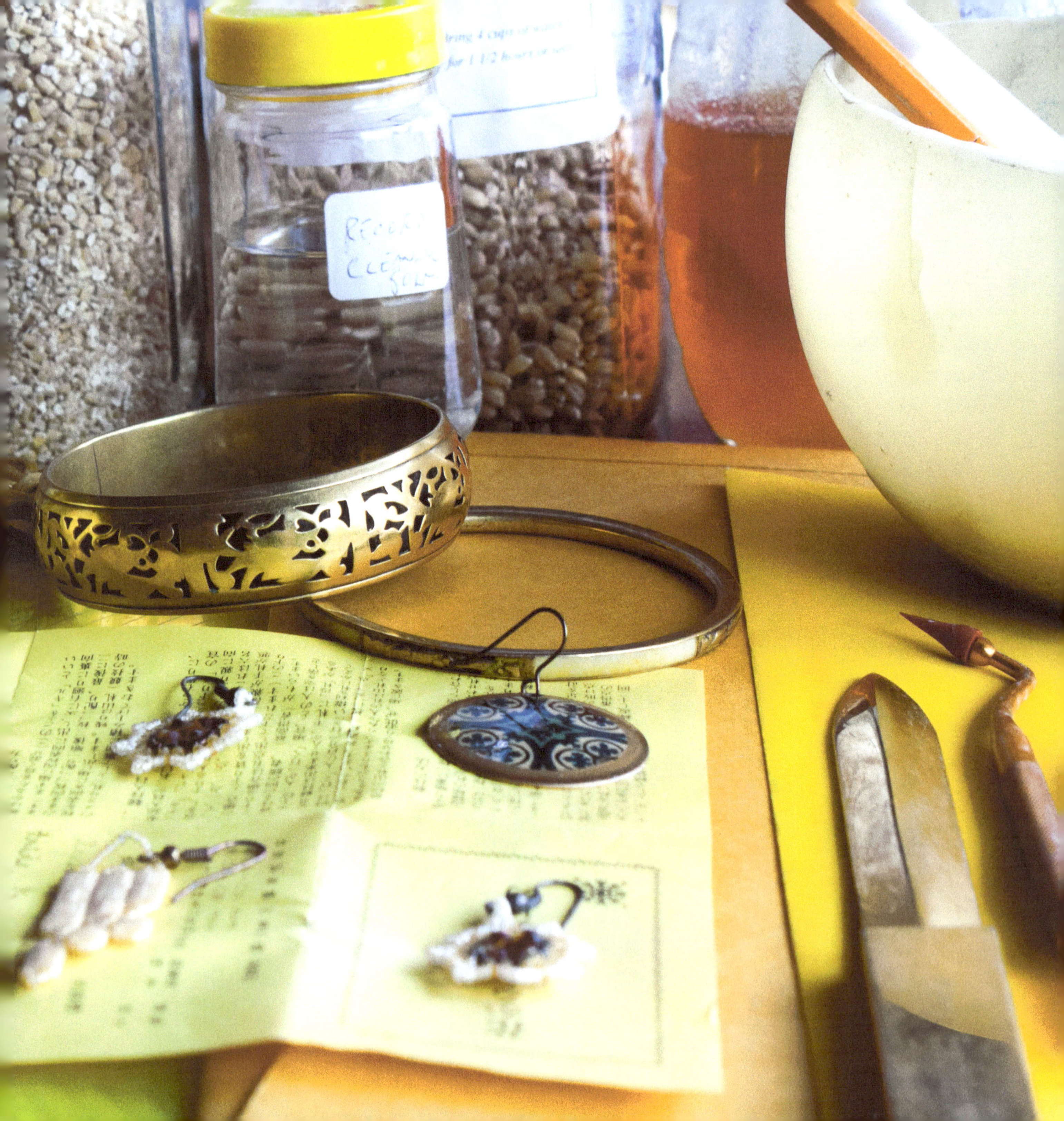

THE HAUNTED WALLPAPER

There are always new shoots on the fungus, and new shades of yellow all over it. I cannot keep count of them, though I have tried conscientiously.

It is the strangest yellow, that wallpaper! It makes me think of all the yellow things I ever saw—not beautiful ones like buttercups, but old foul, bad yellow things.

But there is something else about that paper—the smell! I noticed it the moment we came into the room, but with so much air and sun it was not bad. Now we have had a week of fog and rain, and whether the windows are open or not, the smell is here.

It creeps all over the house.

I find it hovering in the diningroom, skulking in the parlor, hiding in the hall, lying in wait for me on the stairs.

It gets into my hair...

Such a peculiar odor, too! I have spent hours in trying to analyze it, to find what it smells like.

It is not bad—at first, and very gentle, but quite the subtlest, most enduring odor I ever met. In this damp weather it is awful, I wake up in the night and find it hanging over me...The only thing I can think of is that it is like is the COLOR of the paper! A yellow smell...

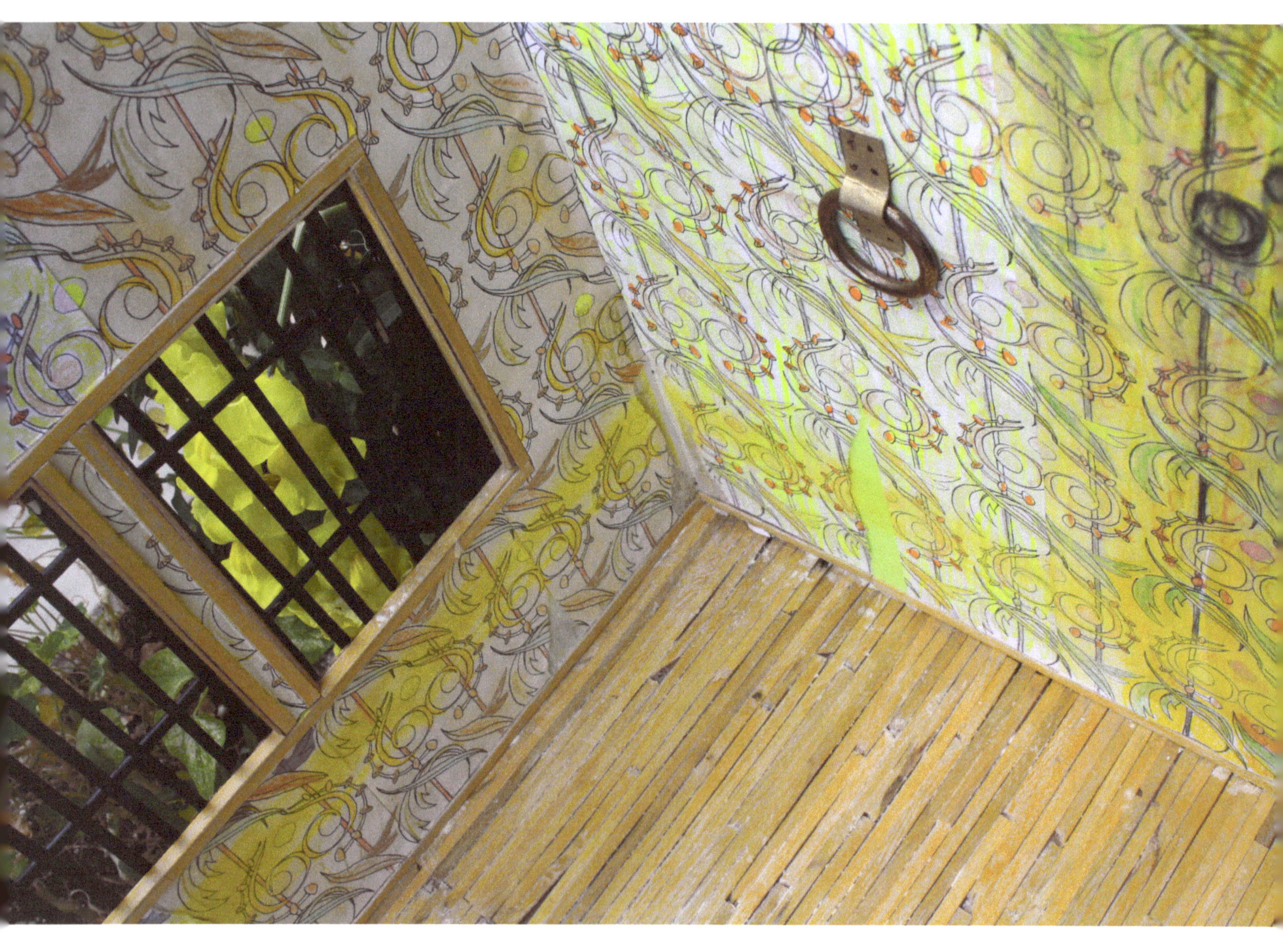

CONTAINED BY A FIELD OF YELLOW

Out of white, carried by the rays of the noonday sun down to the pale salt pan. The egg breaks and reveals its yellow. *Wept at the thought that some would be dyed yellow and some black.* And the yellow cup of the narcissus set in the saucer of the cream white outer petals.

The late August sun spreading over the table like butter on toast, like honey on toast. Start with the sentence, I love this color, and what emerges. Honey falling from the sky. Scrimming off with a small blade a strip of peel from a lemon, breaking those oily cells in the skin, the sharp—spreading a flat blade of butter onto the long rows of corn kernels so that it melts into the crevices. *Pineapple rock, Lemon Platt, Butter Scotch.* Butter in the churn, gold in the miser's chest. Bela told me that the name of this flower was butter and eggs.

Yellow is in the center, the Chinese emperor, and radiates from the center outward, like a sun or a lamp or a daisy. That is its motion. I feel like I am watching at its periphery when I think of it.

Colors are qualities and then pure fields. In the mind they move in and out, a lemon to a river of yellow, that light yellow with a slight green tinge, to a river of light, to down pouring sun, to a time of day, to a mood of mellowness and stillness, to a blond stain over everything, to an even mellower ochre, to that ochre squeezing out of a tube and onto a palette, to the outlines in the murals of Kerala, to a ball of dried mango urine in the Forbes Library of Pigments. Seeing yellow is useful for spotting a poison frog, a crouching leopard, a golden apple, but why can I close my eyes and drown in yellow?

When I was in kindergarten, we were told to make a collage for each color, starting with this one. Color vision first emerged with the spiny sharks in the Carboniferous Period, according to their *fossilized eyes.*[1] A girl in a yellow raincoat, a banana, a daffodil. A bowl of saffron rice and a cloudless sulphur butterfly. That collage was a life changing experience. To hold contained such disparate entities, large, small, plant, creature, all within one yellow force field.

In his study of the still life *Objects on a Table,* Guy Davenport traced the connection between the enigmatic empty cityscapes of early De Chirico with the "true novelty" of the late writings of Nietzsche, both in the city of Turin. De Chirico wrote:

> *This novelty is a strange and profound poetry, infinitely mysterious and solitary, which is based on the* Stimmung *(I use this very effective German word which could be translated as atmosphere in the moral sense), the* Stimmung, *I repeat, of an autumn afternoon, when the sky is clear and the shadows are longer than in summer…I began to paint subjects in which I tried to express the strong and mysterious feeling I had discovered in the books of Nietzsche: the melancholy of beautiful autumn days, afternoons in Italian cities.*[2]

Although Davenport does not say the word, all through his chapter on "the metaphysical light in Turin," I see that light's yellow color.

For most colors, one can reasonably propose a binary of symbolic meanings (white: purity and death; red: love and war). So for yellow: madness and lucidity. Those months in Turin ended when Nietzsche embraced the beaten horse and succumbed to syphilitic derangement. *The outside pattern is a florid arabesque, reminding one of a fungus. If you can imagine a toadstool in joints, an interminable string of toadstools, budding and sprouting in endless convolutions*—What is your relationship to yellow? Matthew: When I think about the color, I don't like it. It makes me think of bodily fluids, pollution, aging.

Citrus sulphur mustard pollen and the gold dust blew away and Humphrey Bogart went insane.

A DREAM OF VIOLENCE

Through some rare balance of forces, a large Victorian hotel has remained suspended above the town for months. Right now it's above the school. As I'm watching a hang-glider sail past, I think, surely someone has gone in to explore it. But then I remember, of course they haven't, since we all know that the slightest shift in weight could bring the whole building down. And just as I think this, the hang-gliding man detaches from his sail and jumps into the hotel through an open window.

And the hotel tips, and sinks, and sure enough, it's coming down to rest on the school, which is starting to buckle under the weight. No school today but that doesn't guarantee the building is empty. As I look for people through the falling plaster and rooms turning to rubble, I encounter the man who caused all of this, setting down a burlap sack. I found the gold! he crows. Wait till the guys see this. He goes off to look for his crew. I sort through the bag, which isn't really that heavy. There's one gold bar, then a chunk of something that's clearly pyrite, and many gold painted book ends, still in their packages. What an idiot! How could he endanger people, and valuable public institutions, for this? I start ranting to anyone who will listen, and we all become enraged. When he comes back, someone bends bright new steel rebar into a baseball bat and hits him on the head. Hit him again, hit him like this, I say, demonstrating. And they move exactly as I do, again and again, so that it's like we're whaling on him together. No matter how we hit him, though, he does not stop braying about his gold. Now we've driven a two-by-four through his head and out through his lower chin, made him the new Phineas Gage, and still he brags on and on. Evidently he wasn't using his brain to begin with.

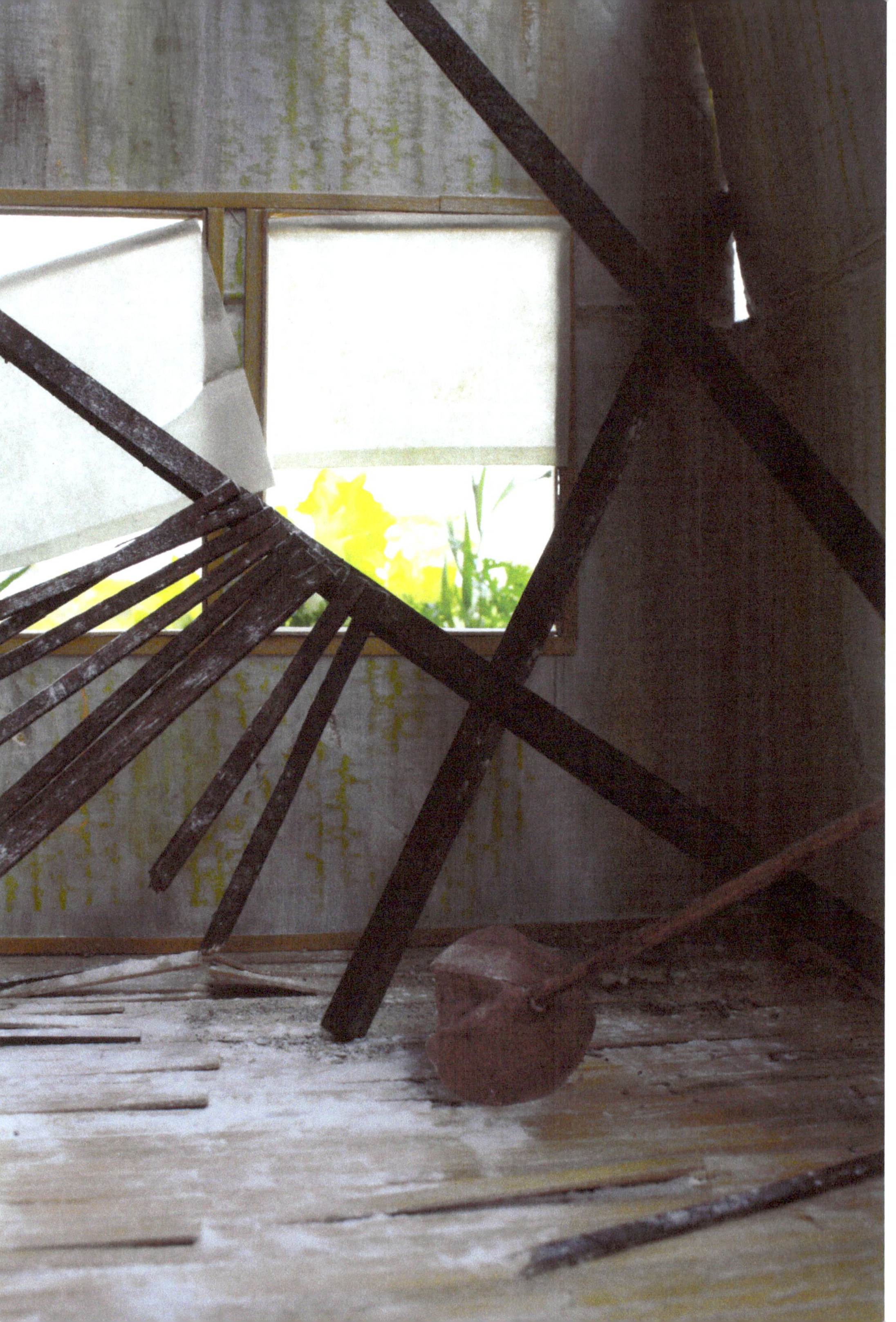

COME CLOSER YELLOW ANIMAL

The Peruvian asp caterpillar, *Megalopyge opercularis,* sports a dramatic upsweep of golden hair.

> According to the scientific literature, contact with the fine hairs—what scientists call 'setae'—is an awful experience. "Intense, throbbing pain develops immediately or within five minutes of contact with the caterpillar"...some patients liken the amount of pain to *a vast image out of Spiritus Mundi troubling my sight: somewhere in sands of the desert a shape with lion body and the head of a man, a gaze blank and pitiless as the sun, is moving its slow thighs, while all about it*
>
> *Reel shadows of the indignant desert birds.* A characteristic grid of bloodcolored spots mark the site of the sting for about a day afterwards...responses to stings "can include headaches, nausea, vomiting, intense abdominal distress, lymphadenopathy, lymphadenitis, and sometimes shock or respiratory stress."[3]

(In the car going home, summer late blue evening, back country road between grassy ditches, and the firefly flashes pour past on either side.)

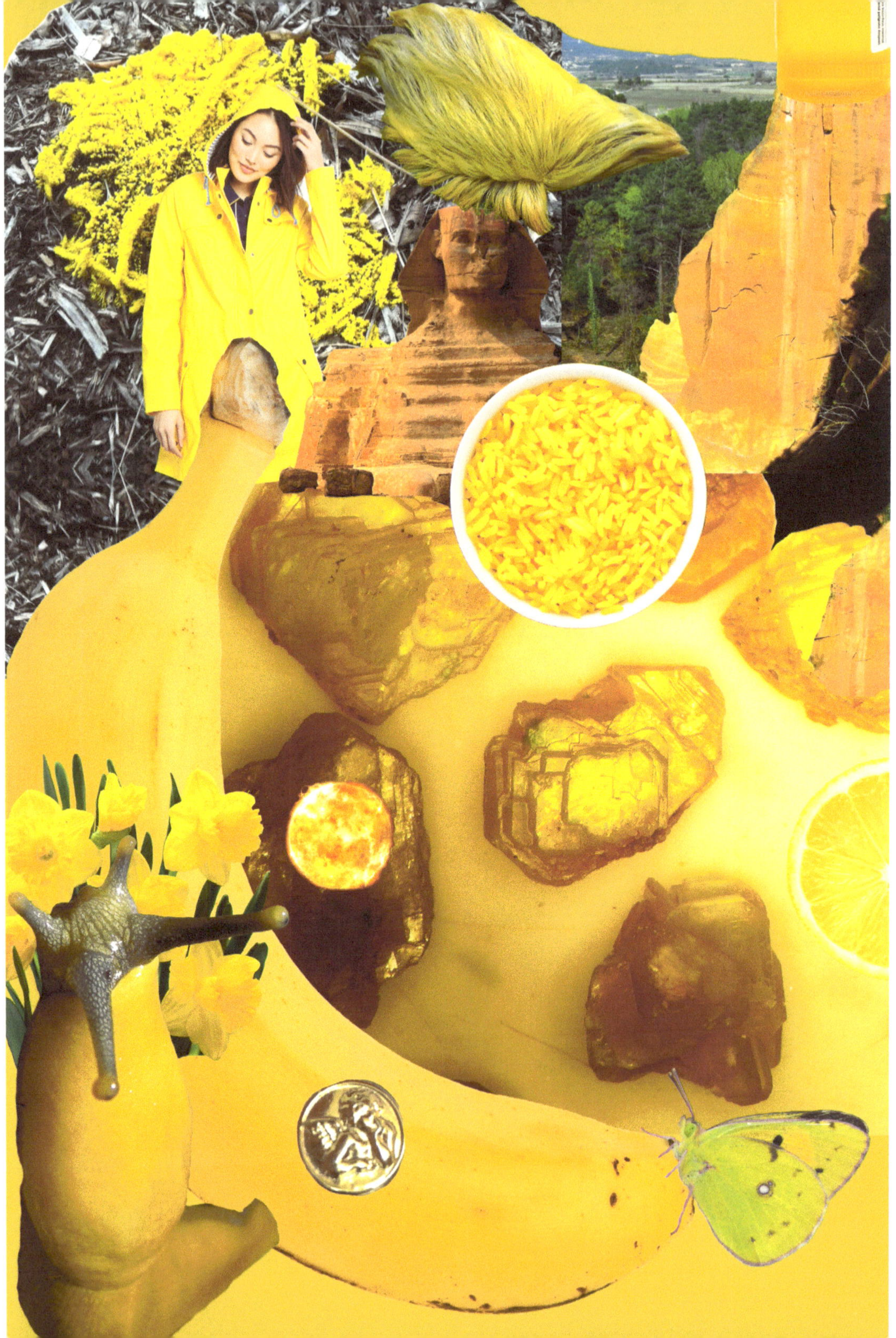

A SUNFLOWER CLOCK

In college, I found myself almost the sole inhabitant of the campus during a spring break. I went out one morning and bought some daffodils. As I was walking back in the rain, the flowers were the only colored thing. Could you not just eat daffodils, to take in that color? I waited for a train to pass, then started across the tracks, the departing train drowning out the sound of the train coming from the other direction. I happened to look up from my flowers into the grey air and the train's screaming face.

Kircher invented the sunflower clock. He put a grown sunflower in a floating planter in the middle of a tub of water marked with the hours. He could never keep the sunflower alive for more than a month, but for that month, whenever it was sunny and without the slightest breath of wind, the clock worked perfectly.[4]

cloth lifted deep yellow from its saffron bath and

a slice of
yellow pound
cake iced with lemon
curd
down
from September mountain sided with aspens to foothills of birches, river banks of cottonwoods, equintoctial fields of goldenrod between the setting sun, the rising moon. Descending on down deep through

the layered canyon walls of the ochre quarries of Roussillon.

Cheap instant macaroni and cheese gets its icteric color from tartrazine, a derivative of coal tar.

When I studied Beowulf in college, the consensus seemed to be that the color terms in that poem reflected a greater concern with light and dark than with precise hues—perhaps the Anglo-Saxons did not bother to name hues as we do, or even notice them. This idea has been contested in the ensuing decades. The biological structures to register color were all there, after all, and most of the time people do not go around naming all the colors they can see. It is manifestly true, though, that there are few colors in the poem. And it also seems to be true that the gold treasures are there for their gleam rather than their yellow.

The gold of Japanese screens brought some dim gleam into the dark open interiors of Heian era mansions. In the compositions of the screens, the gold in the backgrounds functions as white does—mist, sky, snow, as if its shine translated into white.

> Another attraction in Kircher's museum was the 'Catropic theatre'... which he built in emulation of one at the Villa Borghese. It is basically a box lined with mirrors that multiply the images of whatever is on the horizontal table [inside]. This in turn is one side of a parallelipiped, which can be turned by the handle... to present different spectacles. Kircher says that it so amazes viewers that they try in vain to touch what they see inside it. Greedy folk, especially, try to grab the coins [shown in the illustration—the Catropic theatre seems in this case to contain coins], but recoil with groans and indignation when they find them to be insubstantial phantasms.[5]

Short summer night: a gold coin not yet lost—the fox moon.[6]

Pastourea says the Middle Ages was a long argument about the nature of color. Was it light, and therefore akin to the divine, or base matter?[7] Finlay describes how, in Val Camonica full of petroglyphs, she found an odd pebble, "a dirty pale brown stub of clay-like earth about the size and shape of a chicken heart… But when I placed the thumb and first two fingers of my right hand over those three small planes," the pebble revealed itself to be a prehistoric ochre crayon, leaving a mark "the color of a haystack."[8]

Match head against sandpaper, the sulphur bite in the nostrils, and lift up the little yellow flower to the fat bellied, arrow tormented horse of Lascaux.

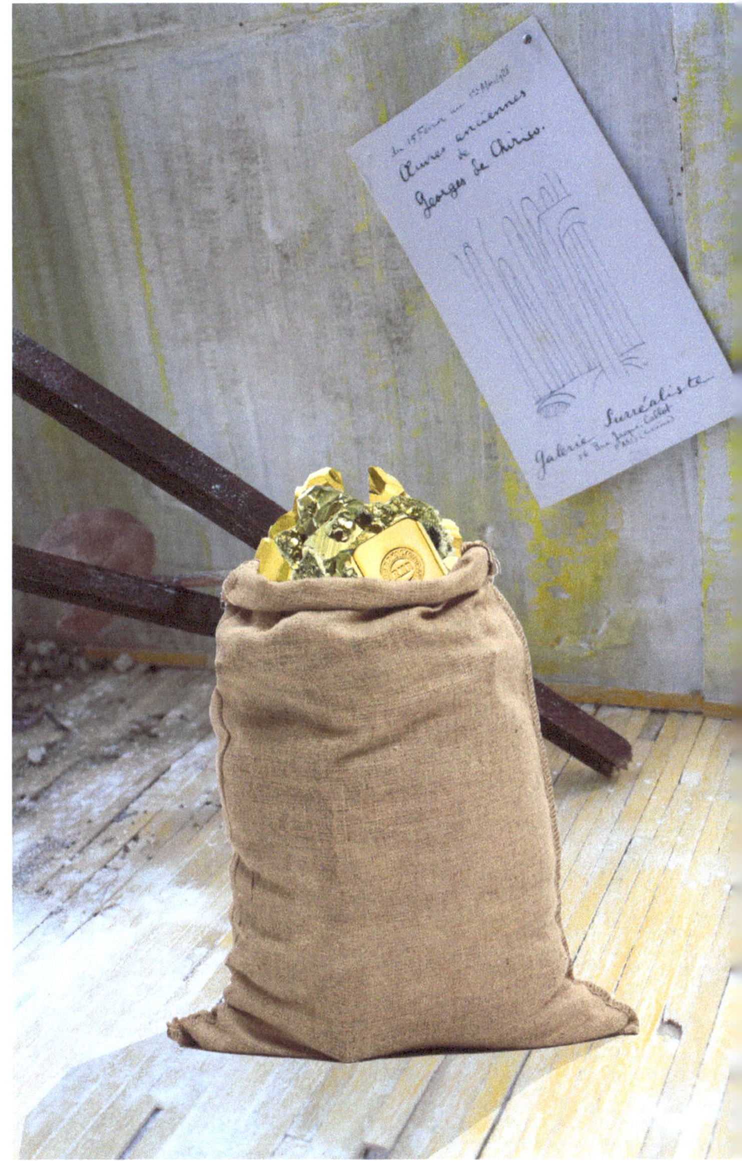

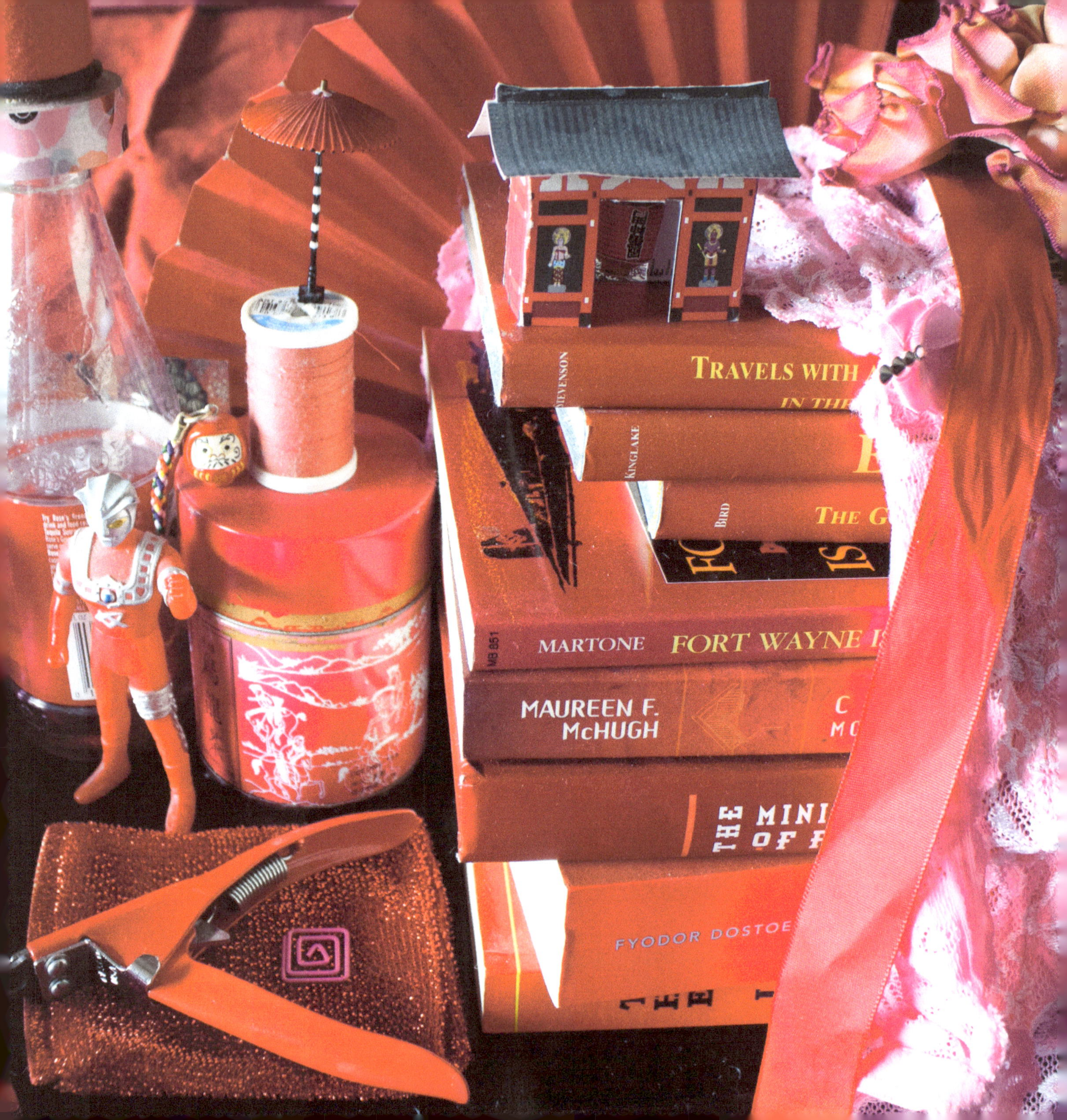

STEVENSON
TRAVELS WITH
KINGLAKE
BIRD
MARTONE
FORT WAYNE
MAUREEN F.
McHUGH
THE

JANE EYRE'S ALCOVE

The child Jane Eyre took a book into the alcove of the breakfast room and drew close the red curtains. Enjoying the respite from the family that had excluded and tormented her, and curtained off from the larger room, she looked out on the grey wind and rain of a late November afternoon. As she looked at the plates of the book, she conjured up in her mind's eye a masterpiece of creative mis-reading: half-informed pictures of the desolate islands off of Norway, of glaciers and Arctic wastes. The rain was too uncomfortable to go out in, so she took her isolation and protection to project upon them scenes of even greater isolation and hardship. Within the cave of the self, we study our minds' projections of the world without, projections that we have edited and exaggerated and embellished to suit our own various purposes.

Red creates an elision in my inaccurate memory: The curtains opened onto the haunted red bedroom where she was sent to be punished and lost her wits. There the mirror showed her as if she were a ghost, her white face and arms floating out of the dim room. The projected light moving up the wall seemed to be the ghost of her uncle and she fainted in terror that he was coming to redress her wrongs. Like the woman in the room with yellow wallpaper, she projected her mind onto the wall. Mechanical reflections and deflections are transmuted through the subject position into seemingly supernatural manifestations. The bourgeois interior is constructed around the fantasy that a dwelling's rooms can be an extension of the self, but the fantasy can terrify by seeming to come true.

But I think the passages in Brontë are also haunting because they acknowledge that red is the color of the self. This is why only red has an autobiography. And *stiff the red landscape where his cattle scraped against Their hobbles in the red wind.*

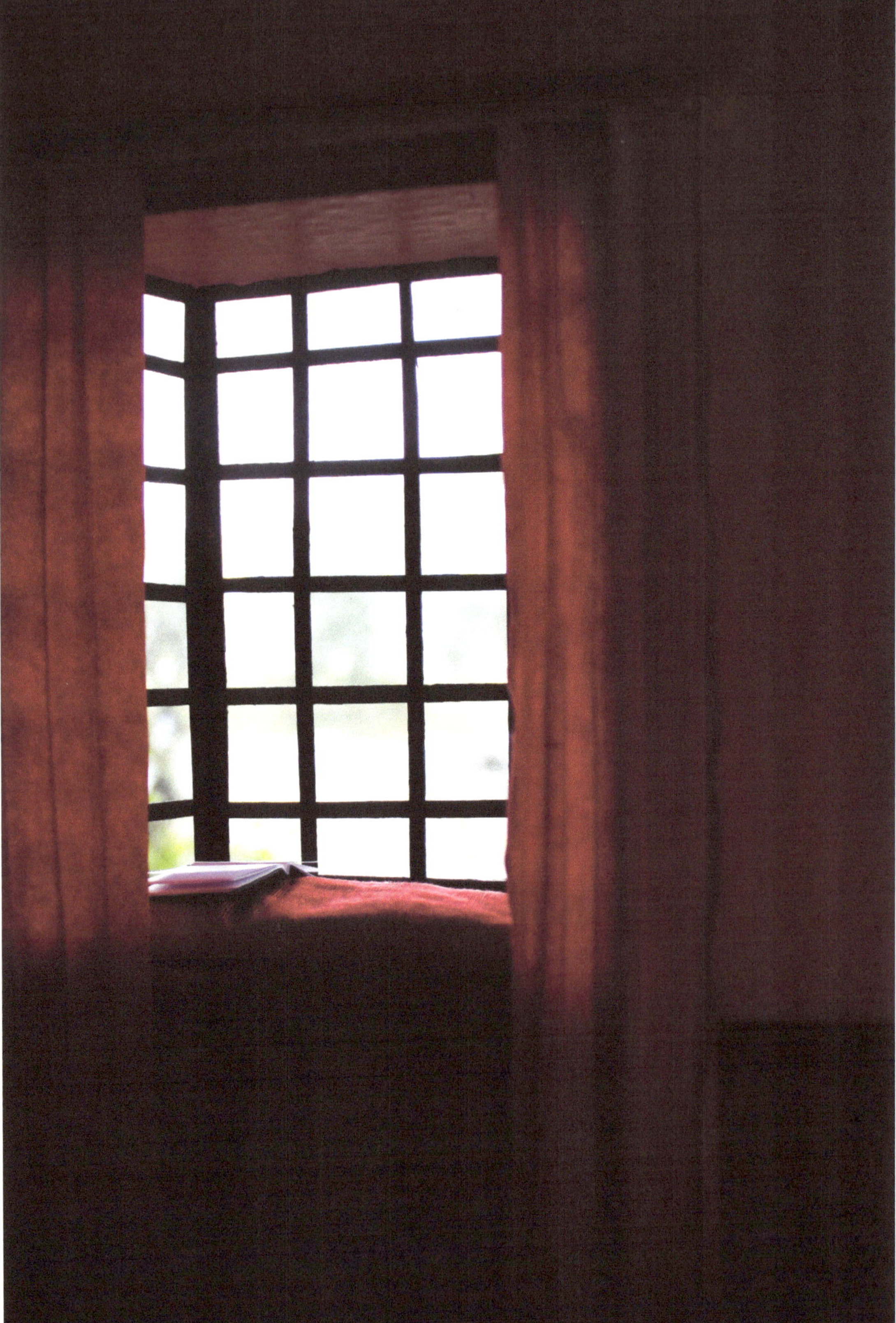

RED ORGANIZES EVERYTHING AROUND ITSELF

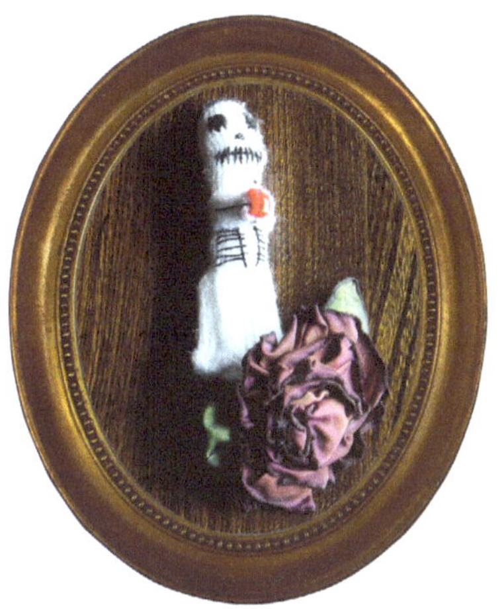

Berlin and Kay's *Basic Color Terms: Their Universality and Evolution* states that when a language has two basic color terms, they correspond to black and white; when a language has three color terms, the next one is always red.[1] So red emerges from the unnameable like the self emerges from the mirror. Why is this? To name the color of blood? A lot of mammals, both predators and prey, cats, dogs, rabbits, don't even have the cones to distinguish red.

Black, white and red, says Pastoureau, the medieval triad of the symbolic order: ebony hair, snow white skin, blood red lips.[2] Another theory about our sensitivity to red is that it evolved to read each other's blushes and rages.

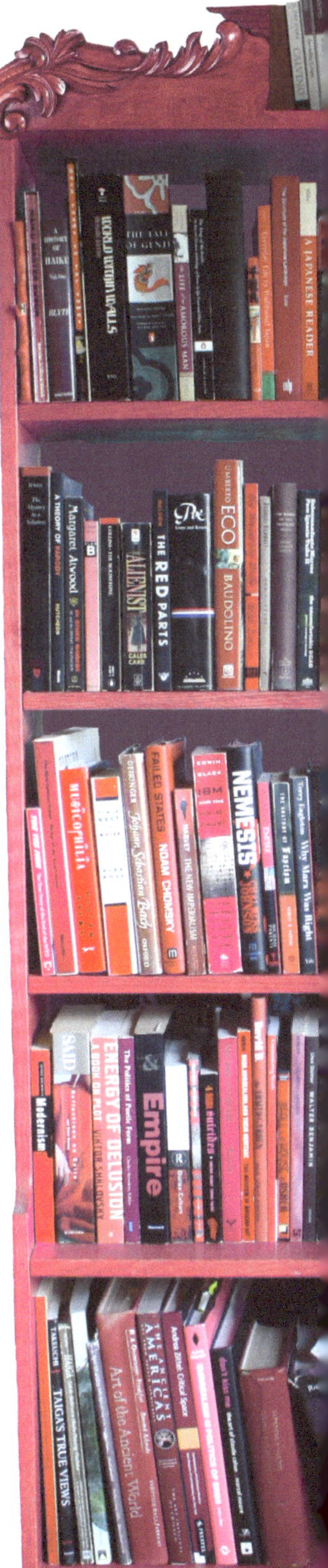

Look at the gods of the Greek pantheon, a realm to each. The god of war, the goddess of love, the god of the sea, the goddess of the hunt. It's not that they negate each other, although they do often fight. It's not as though Aphrodite's worship eliminates war (in fact, Aphrodite likes Ares quite well). Each is a lens through which the world is organized around different elements. If you belong to Aphrodite, as Paris does, erotic love is the emphasized thing, the central thing. When Paris is about to get killed in battle, Aphrodite plucks him out, carries him through the air, and deposits him in Helen's bed.

When I was five, I owned a unique and amazing red umbrella. My mother just handed it to me, at the beginning of the school year, as if it already belonged to me—part of its miracle was that I did not have to pine for it or beg for it first. It came to a pagoda point at the top, like a carousel, and had many ribs and a ruffle around the edge. I was walking home one windy March day, and the wind lifted me up by the umbrella and carried me for about five feet in the air. For months afterwards I ran around in the wind with the umbrella, trying to repeat the experience, but the umbrella only blew inside out until it was quite ruined.

■

But a color is hard to see if it is everything. *The red world And corresponding red breezes Went on*. Better to give a color its proper setting, so that we can experience it with the highest possible charge. So a red dream is not necessarily all red, but it leads to red, it points to red, it revolves around red. Red centers and is the center of the composition.

I'm in a shining white supermarket, talking to some young women, a customer and some people who work there. One clerk gets meat for the customer and hands it to me to wrap up (I guess I work there too). I walk around looking for plastic wrap, but it's hard to find, because now the supermarket is a shining white purveyor of office supplies. I keep forgetting the flopping slab of liver and holding it to my red shirt, but fortunately the blood stains won't show. Copy machines, copy machines, no plastic wrap and the meat is drying out against my shirt.

So I got a red t-shirt, stained it with red food coloring, blew up a red balloon for the meat [I thought a water balloon would have better heft, but I couldn't get it big enough] and stained a paper towel with fake blood, although the food coloring would have worked just as well. Then I prevailed upon my disgruntled husband to pose with these things. Because I have to take the picture, don't I, and really, it doesn't matter if I'm in it or not. This dream, like most of my dreams, isn't about me; I'm just kind of loosely, casually hanging out in the subject position. Substitute anyone.

Then I photoshopped a cow's liver in place of the balloon. No cow was harmed in the making of this picture. But the finished image troubles me in another unexpected way—as if Bobby were walking around holding his own liver. When Batchelor describes the unbroken egg of the art critic's minimalist white house, he cites Bakhtin: The classical body allows for no extrusions, no poking out of insides.[3] Please be careful with that.

Plato tethered the immortal soul in the head, where it is protected by the narrowness of the neck from contamination by the mortal soul, located in the torso. There the better part of the mortal soul is in the upper torso, and the baser, more animalistic part is lower down, "between the midriff and the boundary toward the navel." Then the gods made the liver so that the upper mortal soul could influence the base mortal soul, so bestial and alinguistical, by projecting images upon the liver's shiny red surface. "The force of the thoughts sent down from the mind might be stamped upon it as upon a mirror that receives the stamps and returns visible images." These images on the mirror of the liver, bitter or sweet, teach the lower soul self control and graciousness.[4]

A PERSONAL RED THEATER

My room is a window seat in a little red alcove. At all times a movie is projected onto the window curtain. And I usually watch it; I am now. But the attendant, a small pot-bellied man with grey hair, thoughtlessly closes the curtains in front of the alcove. They're hardly curtains, more like a *noren*, or a banner for a birthday party; they hide little but block off the projection. I'm trying to watch the movie here, I complain as I open them again.

A simple dream but it opens up as I think about it. For one thing, this is certainly a version of Jane Eyre's nook with its red curtains, and with the little personal movie for her book of prints. For another, it reads like my own personal iteration of Plato's cave. I think I am watching the movies in isolation, that they are projections from within my own personality, but then this man blocks the projector and reminds me that they are not in my control and come from elsewhere. Knowing this, I am still irritated that my delusions are disrupted.

A CREATURE DEFINED BY ITS INSIDES

My favorite anecdote from Greenfield's *A Perfect Red* is the young John Donne sailing to the Azores as a cochineal pirate, complaining that:

> *Lighting was all our light, and it rain'd more*
> *Than if the Sunne had drunk the sea before.*

But they bore red out of the grey storms, capturing three Spanish ships out of Havana and relieving them of their large cargoes of dye. Cochineal flowed from Mexico to Spain, but the English were so successful in stealing it that they bragged it might as well have been arranged for their own benefit, every English aristocrat in red clothes a thumb in the eye of the Spanish.[5]

■

Or outsides. Color terms attest not only to the biological ability to see color, but the color's importance to a culture. Color in *Beowulf* becomes suddenly precise when describing horses, which come in five colors: white, black, chestnut, grey, and *fealawan,* which is perhaps bay or dun or dappled. Hrothgar gives Beowulf four *appelfealuwe* horses, perhaps "tawny like apples."[6]

■

In the hallway of the Seattle youth hostel, an extremely fit young man wearing a red cotton towel was making his way from the showers to his room. Laura and I observed a careful moment of silence as he went by. That was an extremely red towel, I said. Yes, it was a very nice color, said Laura.

Although red is so demanding a presence, it is hard to keep. The history of dyeing could be told by the color red, so desirable and so difficult to sustain that all the dyer's invention went into preventing it from vanishing in the sun and the wash water. And the history of colonialism could be metonymically conveyed by the history of cochineal, full of carminic acid, the most brilliant red dye the world had seen. The insects were raised in nopalries, the legless bumps harvested from the cactus paddles and dried. The Aztecs collected huge quantities of cochineal as tribute, and their markets were full of brilliant red goods—cloth, leather, feathers. In the wake of genocide and disease, it took many years to build up the network of trade and tribute and forced labor that would send bags of dyestuff across the Atlantic. Animal, vegetable—for a long time the Europeans didn't even know what the dried granules were.[7]

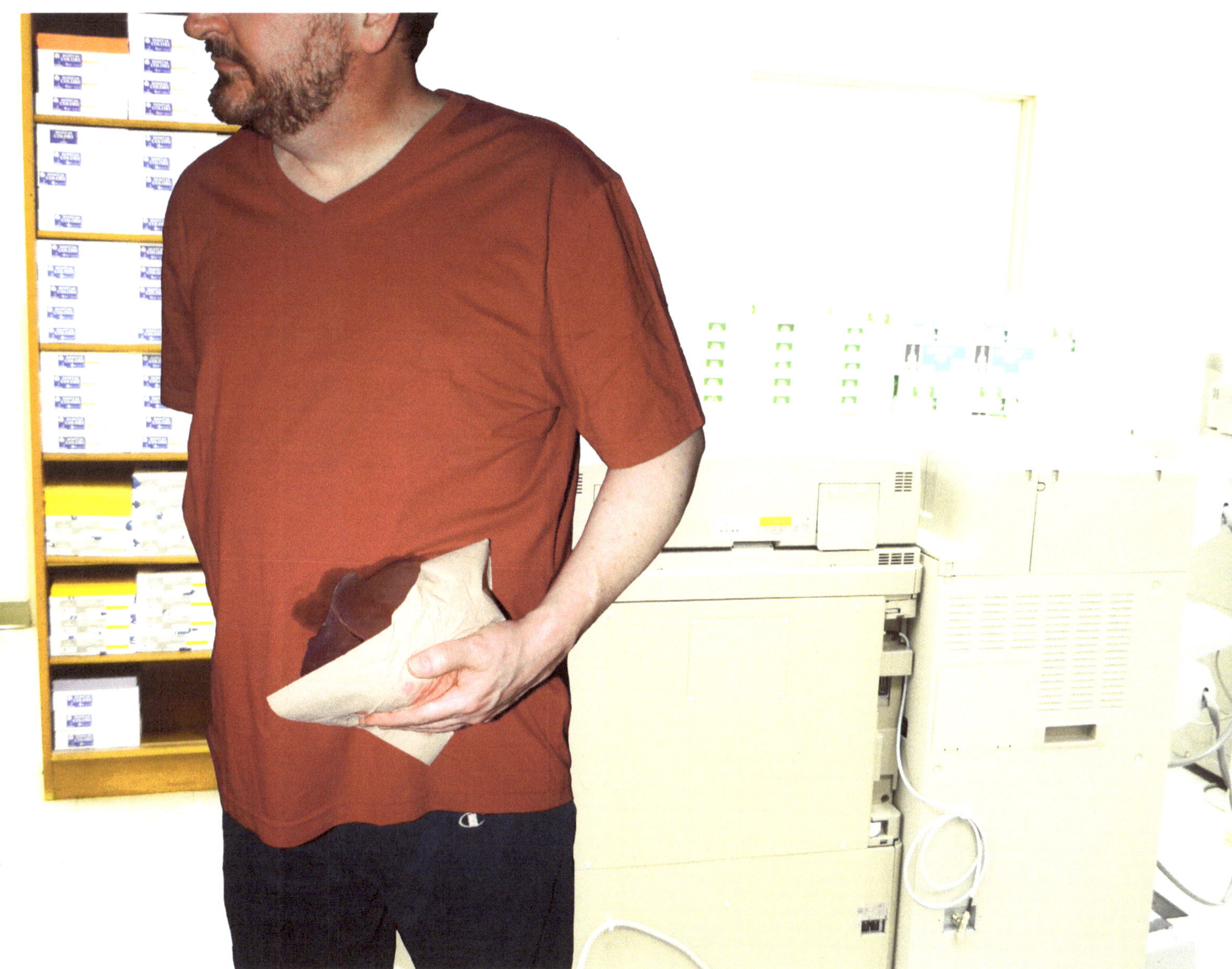

FUGITIVE MADDER LAKE

When I was five, I used to take a shortcut home from school through a field. One fall day next to the path in the middle of the green field there was a burning bush. It was flaming orange pink and its twigs had weird yellow ridges along them. That color stopped my breath. Obviously the bush had been there all along, but I had never noticed it when it was green or bare, so it was as if it appeared out of nothing. To paraphrase Breton's axiom, Tell me what you haunt, and I'll tell you who you are. I haunt that bush in the field. I am still there, and it is still there, flaming salmon red at me like God did to Moses. Question: What makes you feel like you belong in your life, and are not rolling around in it like a loose marble in a box? That, that moment, the memory of that moment, that I got to see that color, that I was there to be *struck* by it.

Colors move between abstract purities and contingent qualities, but sometimes the quality becomes an entity in its own right. I saw a bank of red tulips, so red they were flat, escaped dimension, and felt my own pulse in the quicks of my nails.

Of all the shades of Japanese plum trees, the dark pink were my favorite, blooming in snow, smelling of cloves.

I saw that our neighbor's magnolia tree blooming behind our garage roof was a mountain of rose flowers, something out of a religious allegory.

I saw the petals of the lavender pink resurrection lilies in our yard darken to faintest blue at the tips, lighten to the faintest yellow at the base.

(Roses through intoxication yoke their smell to their rose red. Rosewater, though, hiding at the end of a sip of lassi or a bit of baklava, tastes pale pink.)

(All parts of the burning bush, or winged spindle tree, are mildly poisonous.)

Describe an intense relationship you have with a particular color.

Lucy: What is this nonsense.

For example, your favorite color is red. So do you have stronger feelings for reds that tend toward orange or purple?

Lucy: Oh. Oh. That seems at first like such a hard question. Because purple red, wine red—you want to be surrounded by it, right? You want to swim in it. But orange red is, oh oh like berries, it's like bittersweet berries just showing in flashes, and even though the forest is dull grey, that red arranges it all, it's just everything.

So both kinds of red are equally compelling, then.

Lucy: Of course not—weren't you listening?—of *course* the orange red is better.

Human trichromatic vision does not work the way one would expect. Our sensitivities are not spaced evenly—the red and green receptive cones overlap through most of their range, so we are very good at distinguishing between red and green, or different greens. Possibly this helps us to distinguish ripening fruit from foliage.[8] *At the top of the tree, sick leaves—no, an apple…*[9] The striptease of red. Move slightly and another raspberry reveals itself behind leaves. Come out, rain down upon us, a flood of anthocyanins and carotenoids, edible, inedible, and poisonous together, the lobed rose pink pods of spindle trees, *Herman eaten all the chewwies*, apples, tomatoes, rowan berries, white tipped radishes, cranberries, grapes, holly, winterberry, chokecherry, barberry, clustered garnet pomegranate seeds, smashed open watermelon, blood oranges with their port wine stain. "*More beautiful after the field cleaving wind: pepper's exotic red*."[10]

Owain proposed this question: What, as a child, did you wish to eat, even though you knew you shouldn't?

Translucent yew berries, because of the square hole at the bottom where the green seed shows through.

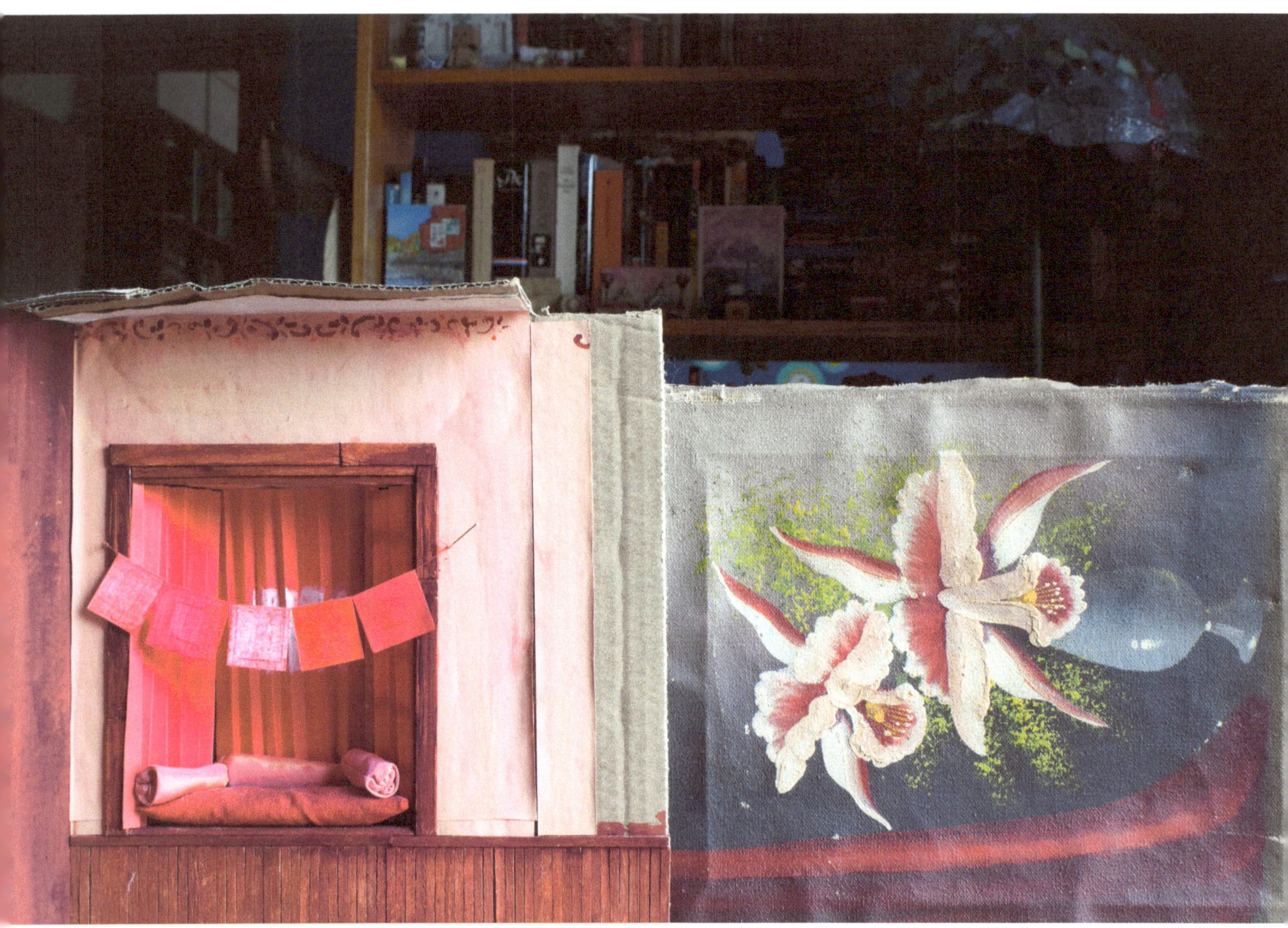

VERMILION AND MERCURY POISONING

A dish of calamine lotion to feed trapped birds. Shards of a broken tail light and the spiny nylon banner of my inside-out umbrella. In the movie version of *The Wizard of Oz*, the silver slippers became ruby slippers to make better use of technicolor. The oldest crayon I can find news of was discovered in northern England. It is not yellow ochre but red. It is 10,000 years old, beveled at one end to come to a point, and an inch long.[11]

Arnoux has now become a pottery merchant and claims he can imitate Chinese red glaze, said Bobby, who was in the middle of *A Sentimental Education*.

According to my reading, that sounds either doubtful or extremely toxic, I said.

He's probably lying. Very dodgy character.

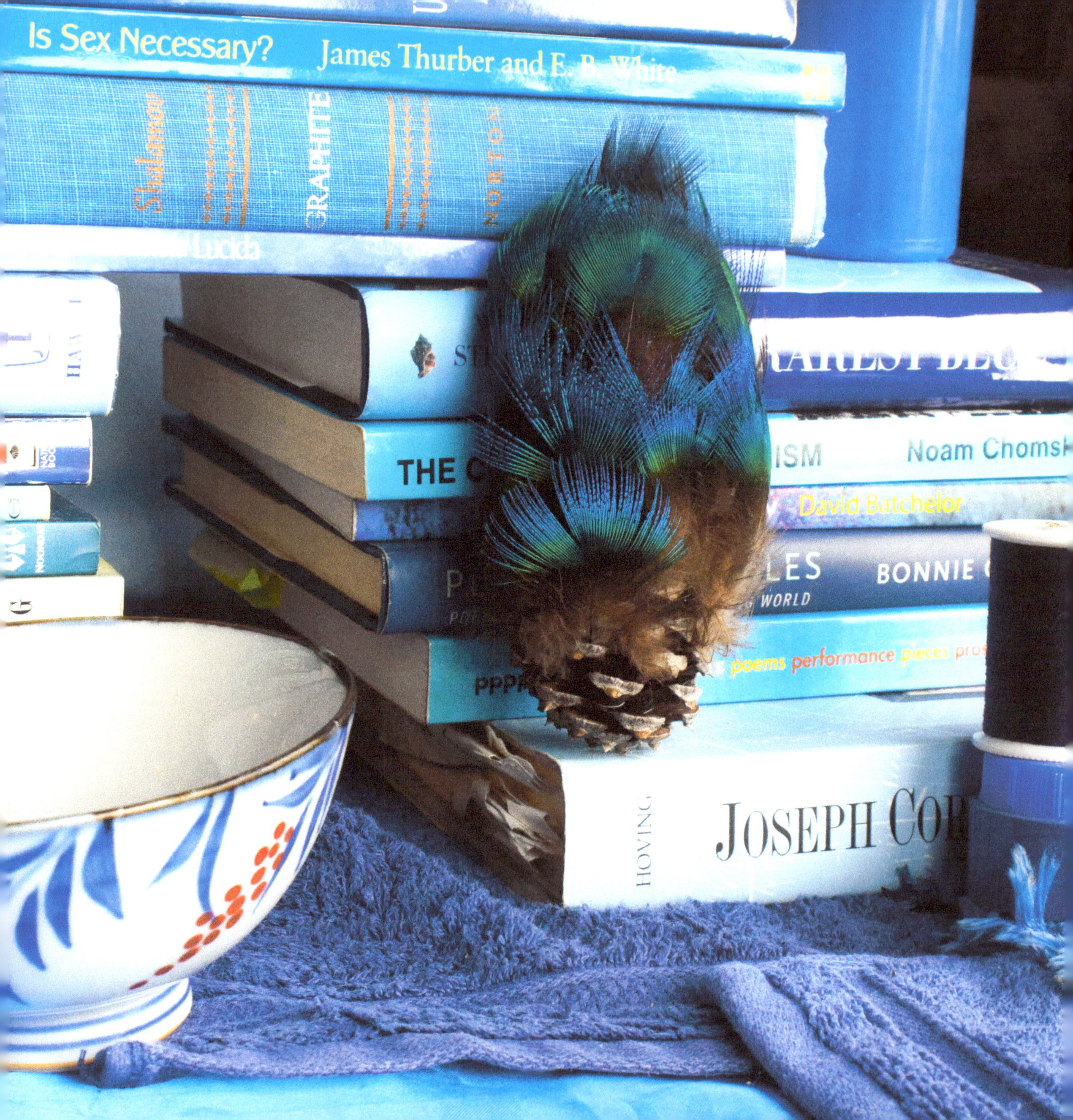
Is Sex Necessary?
James Thurber and E. B. White
GRAPHITE
NORTON
Lucida
THE
Noam
David Batchelor
BONNIE
WORLD
poems performance pieces
HOVING
JOSEPH

CONSTELLATION AS CONSOLATION

Left it for last, but finally, the blue towers of objects covered the table. Needed more light, waited for days until the grey withdrew and the sky emerged. Camera still not cooperating. Ate our meals crammed over on one side of the table so that the blue arrangement might remain undisturbed. I wish we could live like this, as in the front row of the theater, following the rhythm of objects, watching the colors and their dramatic interactions. Bobby complained that there wasn't enough room for the plates. But it's For The Sake Of Art, I said. Fuck Art, he said, equally skilled at capitalization.

THE LOBBY OF THE SKY HOTEL

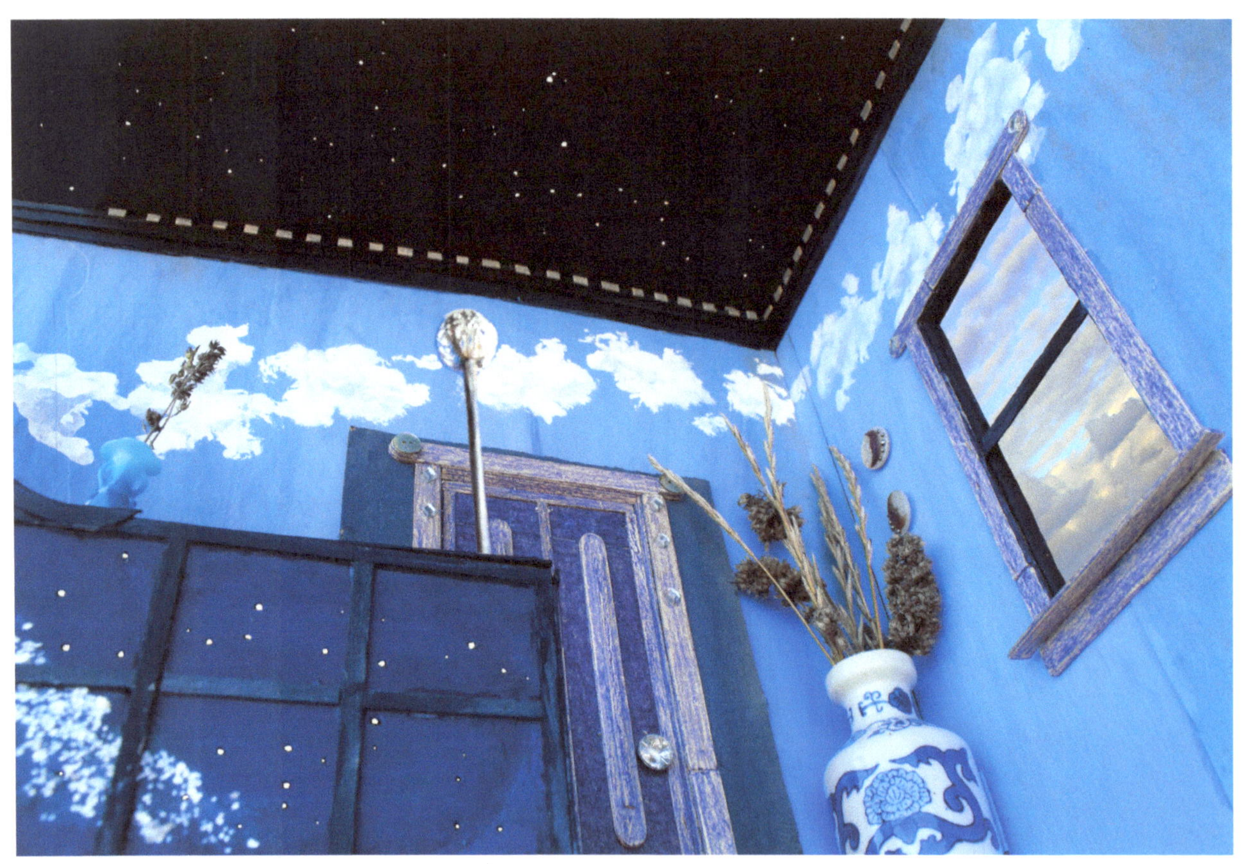

BLUE FLOWS AWAY BEFORE YOU

What smells blue? Behind the green of pine needles, their smell is blue: bracing, even piercing; clean, even antiseptic. The ocean smells more like a green blue, with its rotting kelp. Perhaps the fresh wind on a clear day has a whiff of sky receding behind the grass and exhaust. *Morning glories: each corolla intimate with the color of the abyss.*[1]

I prefer cool rather than hot, night rather than day, moon rather than sun. I thought these preferences made up an identity. But as I stand under the red lamp, and you stand in moonlight from the window, I see that they are instead a catalogue of lacks. They are the things you have and I do not. In this light, I'm life and you're death, and you would think that made me the nice one. But you're the one calmly saying, rest now, it's all right to stop, while I, sweaty and bullying and pink in the face, insist that life must go on and on and on no matter how painful, all to satisfy my endless lust for spectacle. It is better to be you. But perhaps I shift toward blue to you also, as I walk toward your red centered self.

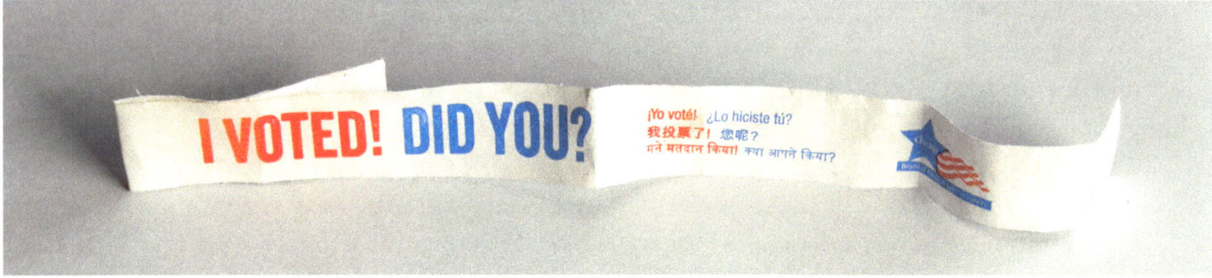

Why in your paintings do you paint everything blue?

Mother: Because everything is blue.

■

Blue recedes, and so does the certainty of its nature. In nature most blue is brought about by structure rather than pigment. The sky has no color, and the sun strikes it with the full spectrum of arrows. But the molecules of air scatter short blue wavelengths of light more effectively than longer wavelengths, as can be so well observed from the lobby of the sky hotel. *All in the blue unclouded weather.* Aquamarine, baby, Capri, cerulean, Egyptian, electric, haint, Klein's, Majorelle, midnight, navy, powder, Prussian, royal, sea, sky, steel, ultramarine, Yin Min. On the walls of the hotel are depicted the reaches of far away. Think of how often we use the inner membrances of our protective shells to look at the outside, not only through windows, but also at paintings of ships at sea. Mountain peaks. Framed old maps.

In human productions, blue is almost always created with artificial agents. On our last vacation, I thought, what is a vacation sort of thing to drink. Blue river soda, and the bit of extra effort it required to take such an unnatural hue into my gullet. I was rewarded, though, with that sugary flavor of generalized imitation fruit, the taste of childhood, with its blue tongue.

■

Berlin and Kay began *Basic Color Terms* after realizing that many languages did not distinguish between blue and green (hence the linguist's term 'grue').[2] Japan's basic color term *aoi* describes the full range of blues and greens (which is why there are so many jade green mountains and blue green willows in early English translations of Japanese poetry).

Whole theories have been built on the color blindness of the ancient Greeks, with their wine dark seas, because Homer did not use a precise term for blue. But why bother to say that the sky is blue?

More pertinent to say that it is clear, or cloudless, or bright. Hue for some peoples is less important than lightness, darkness, matte, shine, emotional tone. And how can we definitively pin down what a basic color term is? And just what conclusions can we draw about a culture, based on its color vocabulary? And how much does language merely reflect, and how much does it actively govern perception? Is there such a thing as a universal experience of color? *Basic Color Terms* has become in the decades since its publication the grounds for ferocious debate.

> In Majid's work with the Jahai of the Malay Peninsula, for example, she would put out a bunch of color chips and ask people to group the chips by which are "similar." "They would take pairs, and put red and blue together, this sort of thing," says Majid. When she and her team asked them why, they would say things like, "Husband and wife go together," she says. Such linguistic difficulties make it very hard to do this kind of work...[3]

In China, wrote Kircher, Lake Chin, full of water lilies (*starred with flashes*), covered the ruins of a city destroyed by earthquake. Amid the lilies floated a raft that bore the disaster's only survivor, the abandoned child.[4]

THE ALCHEMICAL KEY

A lapis lazuli crayon that I am using to draw from memory an alchemical key, draw in an absolutely saturated color. The key will now be revealed to the world! Ringed at the top, small key shaft sticking out of the end, the middle a long solid rectangle, as if it contains something no one is permitted to see.

Bobby tells me he dreamed the same night that he is about to inoculate himself with a syringe. He and the doctors he works for have passed around the syringe, each supposed to inject a few drops, but he has stalled the whole thing, holding the needle to his skin, demanding, what's IN this thing, anyway? And now I realize that my key is much more like the outline of an old fashioned syringe, with a ring on the top of the plunger.

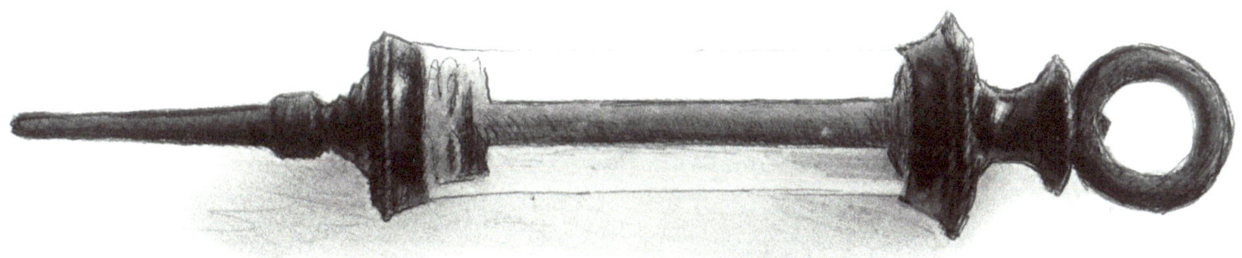

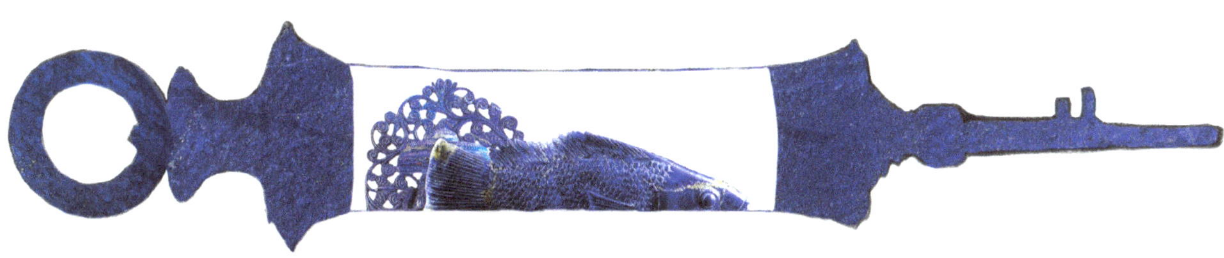

BLUE FOOT FETISH

Blue animals do occur, but animals, like the sky, usually take a short cut and create the color structurally. Peacocks, blue jays, morphos—grind up the feathers or scales, and there's only brown dust. A layer of keratin structures and air pockets in the blue jay's feathers scatters the blue light, while the brown melanin below that is the feather's true pigment absorbs the other colors.

One exception is the actually blue feet of the blue footed booby. Being able to make the difficult blue pigment is such an advertisement for abundant health that their feet figure prominently in their mating dances. The booby fixes his eyes on the female of his dreams and slowly, intently, lifts one large turquoise webbed foot, then the other. Lookee here. The more blue his foot, the more powerful his allure. The female, if she accepts his overtures, lifts her feet also. Once bobbies have mated, their blue fades—too much energy to put into something no longer necessary.

When gathering its nesting materials, "The satin bowerbird, *Ptilonorhynchus violaceus,* specializes in blue objects and has been known to favor blue ballpoint pen tops, blue bottle tops and blue drinking straws."[5]

I once had a dream that Bobby could turn himself at will into a husky with his own blue eyes (handsome dog). And, perhaps in answer, he dreamed of a blue dog. His description of this dream dog bedizened with lucky charms was quite the offering; what could I do but slowly raise my faded blue foot in voluptuous salute.

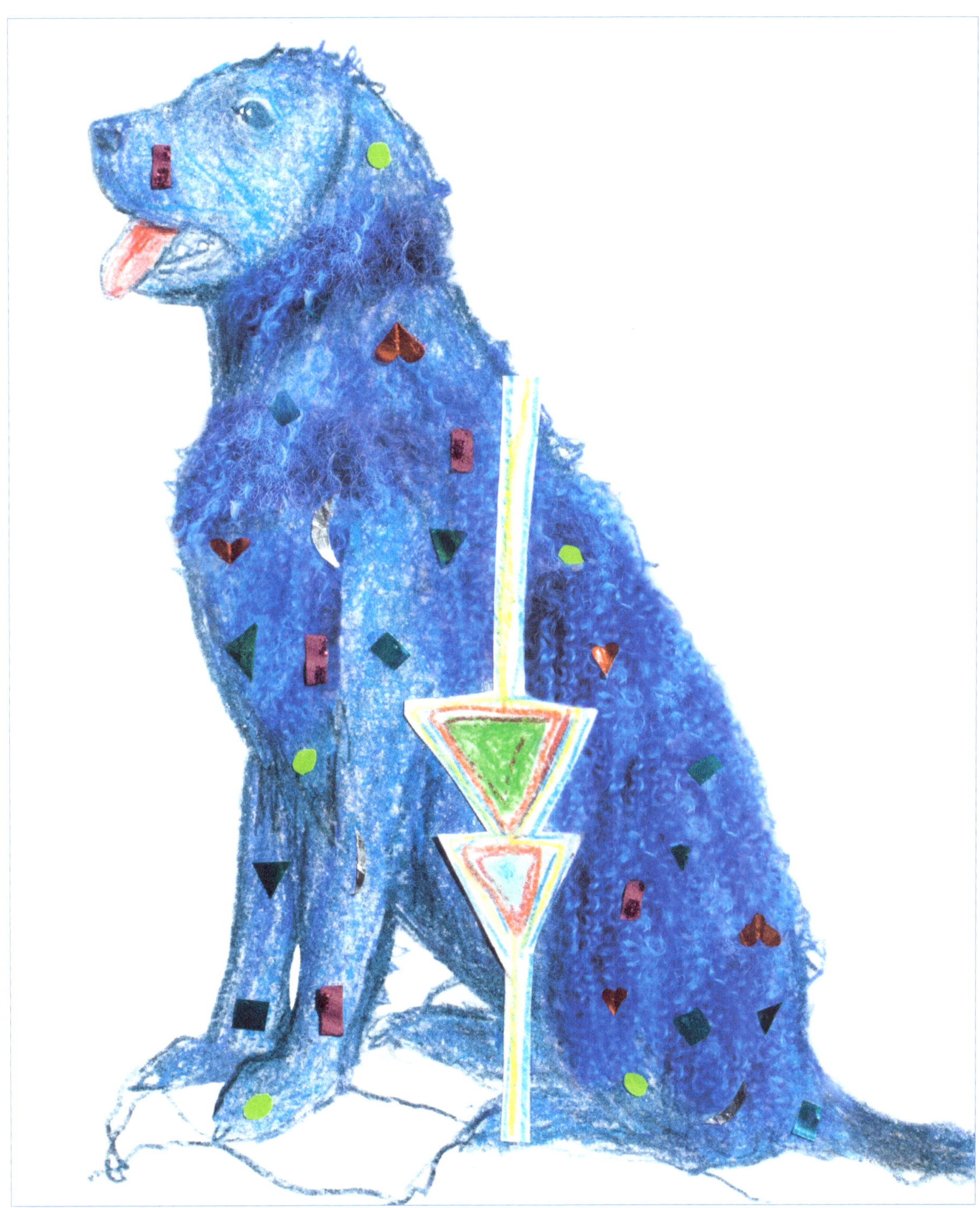

INDIGO INTERVIEW

A small flower from the asparagus family blooms early in the spring, just after the snowdrops, still soon enough to be a surprise. Its racemes of six petaled flowers hang down, each intense lavender-blue petal striped with a deeper violet blue. Its stamens and anthers are dark blue as well.

I was seven or eight, and there was a gap between our garage and the neighbor's that allowed us to slip secretly into the shaded recesses of their back yard, where no one could see us. One spring evening, the neighbor's garden under yew trees was crowded with these flowers that in the dim light seemed luminous, impossible. Their name, I learned long afterwards, is Siberian squill. Siberian! Perfect: cold lonely distant mysterious, but then… squill. I miss the nameless flowers, which seemed to exist in private relation to me.

(Writing this book is teaching me how many flowers are poisonous. Siberian squill, exuberantly invasive, is avoided by all animals but bees. Its red sister is a major ingredient in rat poison.)

Occasionally something will circle back to those blue flowers. At thirteen, I tried to make an illustration for *The King of Elfland's Daughter.* I took great pains with the human figures, the prince and the elf princess, as they crossed the twilight barrier out of Elfland; I composed a deep and detailed background of forest and spires. But it was all to frame the farthest background of forget-me-not blue mountains. What foreground would give the proper context to that color? Really I would have loved to paint a canvas that blue and call it a day. Now the book reads as precious and mannered, but certain passages make clear why I was so drawn to it.

> *Know then that in Elfland are colors more deep than are in our fields, and that the very air there glows with so deep a lucency that all things seen there have something of the look of our trees and flowers in June reflected in water. And the color of Elfland, of which I despaired to tell, may yet be told, for we have hints of it here; the deep blue of the night in Summer just as the gloaming has gone, the pale blue of Venus flooding the evening with light, the deeps of the lakes in the twilight, all these are hints of that color.*

Studying dyes and pigments is a profound lesson in dialectical materialism. When indigo began to be imported to England, the local woad growers, protecting their industry, spread the lie that indigo dye was poisonous.

Have you studied the history of indigo dyeing?

Veronique: As a botanist, I am very interested in this. There is only one natural blue dye, only slight variants on a single blue molecule, but it shows up in different, often unrelated plants. In Europe it is in *bourre,* or woad as you say in English (also it is called *pastel,* like the crayon). In India it is in indigo, in Japan in dyer's knotweed, in South America in anil, elu in Nigeria. It is even part of the color from the snails, the murex. So all over the world people have learned to extract this dye from the source they have available to them. And of course, to use, it is like magic—cloth turns a kind of yellow-green in the vat, and then after a few minutes, you pull it out and the oxygen turns it blue.

Is it harmful to use? Georgia plantations Caribbean slave labor the 1856 Indigo Revolt in Bengal etc. etc.

Veronique: Yes, but those are special circumstances. For most of human history, it has just been a useful plant like many others.

Then she showed me, on the tiny phone screen, her bolts of blue cloth from the Ivory Coast and Mali, marked with white shibori patterns. Lines of conch shells were printed on a damask woven with rows of clustered flowers. (So interesting, she said. The damask pattern is a Louis Quatorze cliché, but then with this bold simple pattern over it.) A feather-like pattern on cotton had been ironed to a high sheen. There were stitched patterns of diamonds where the resist was made from embroidery. She had a piece of Indian *bandhani* where the curved lines of shibori dots were myriad and tiny and the fabric was not ironed so that the wrinkles would prove that the fabric had really been tied off and not just dyed to imitate the method. She explained that midnight blue was only obtained by dipping the cloth into the dye vat many times. There was also a length of crackle patterned batik where the blue was only an interim acquisition, a decorative note on the brown cloth.

FROM THE STADIUM OF CRAYONS

On the other hand, look at all the words for blue derived from minerals: steel, sapphire, turquoise, cyan, phthalo, cobalt, zaffre. Azure is named for the star flecked chunks of lapis lazuli carried by donkey from the valley of Kokcha in Afghanistan to color the ultramarine cloak of the Virgin Mary in Renaissance paintings. Ultramarine: from Latin, meaning 'beyond the sea'—brought from an unimaginable distance. The European painters who valued it so highly had no idea where it came from.[6]

Cellini's recipe for ultramarine pigment: grind then mill down lapis lazuli into a fine but not too fine powder, mix it with melted gum rosin, gum mastic and beeswax, and form it into an extraction stick (and there I see the lapis blue crayon of my dream). After a proper interval, a lowly painter's apprentice would knead the stick for hours in water as the blue seeped from the wax and stained the water into paint.[7]

■

Studying the history of dyes and pigments is a profound lesson in the way people can be poisoned. Cobalt is named for a goblin, because the ore it was smelted from produced arsenic fumes. The mining, the smelting, the poisonous wastes, the transport, the design, the manufacture, the poisonous wastes, the distribution and advertising and investment in stock and display, all so that I can walk down the store aisle and see a blue glass vase and say, it looks like that was *made for me.*

She could not look out the window directly, the Lady of Shallott, and saw the world only *thro' the mirror blue.*

■

At the factory, I see that mice have been trained by the floor supervisor to ferry away the spent cartridges in glass containers set on old roller skates. I follow one mouse to a brimming disposal pit, where it drops off the cartridge and goes to collect more. Why bother with the glass containers when they're just using them to transport the cartridges to an open pit? This is no way to deal with radioactive material! And what about the poor mice? The whole factory stained blue with radiation. *My hope dwindled to a ghost.* We are so doomed

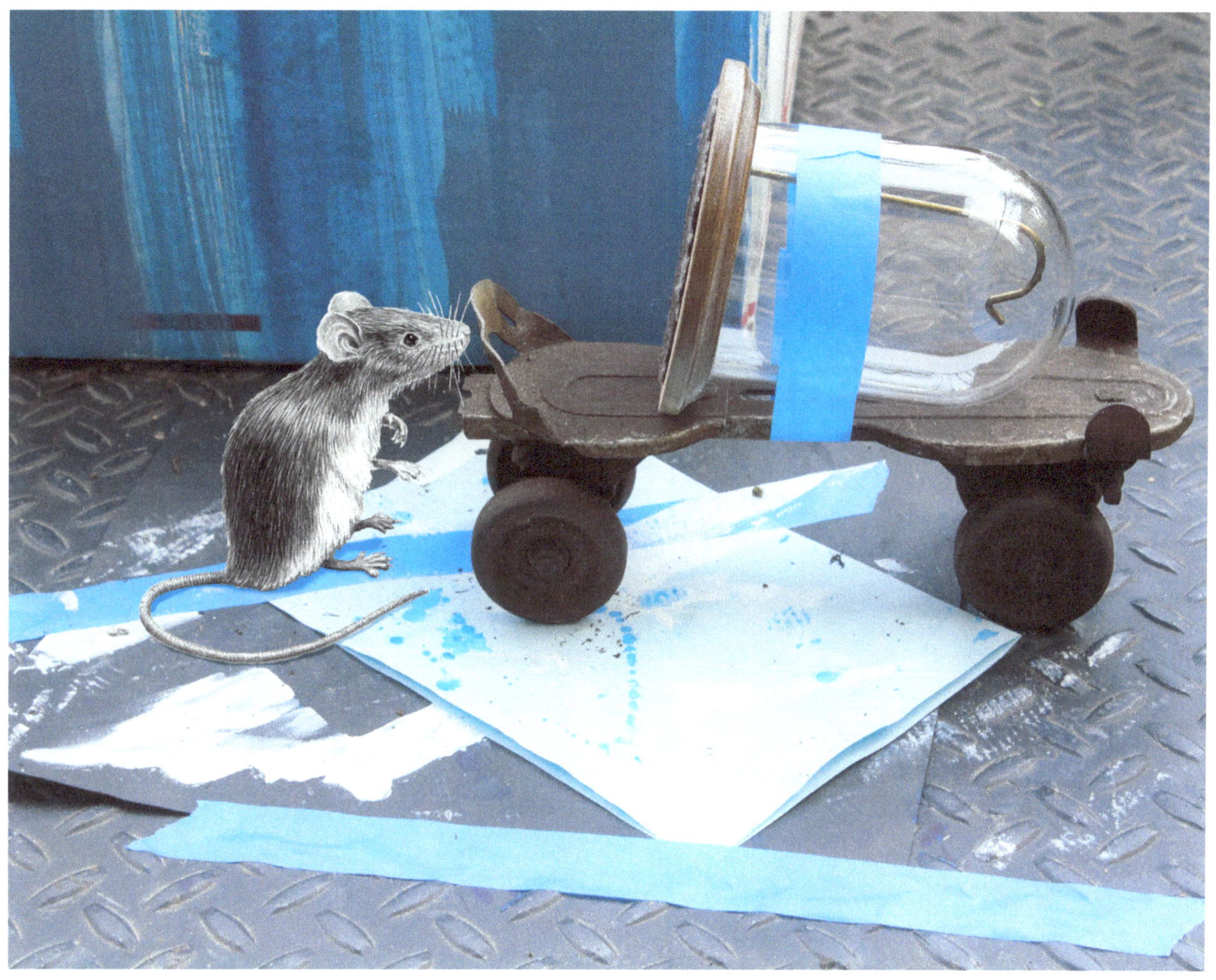

Both ice giants Uranus and Neptune are made blue by their atmospheres of hydrogen, helium and methane, but Uranus is a pale turquoise and Neptune is a much intenser blue. Some additional trace in its atmosphere saturates the color, some element we have *not yet been permitted to see.*

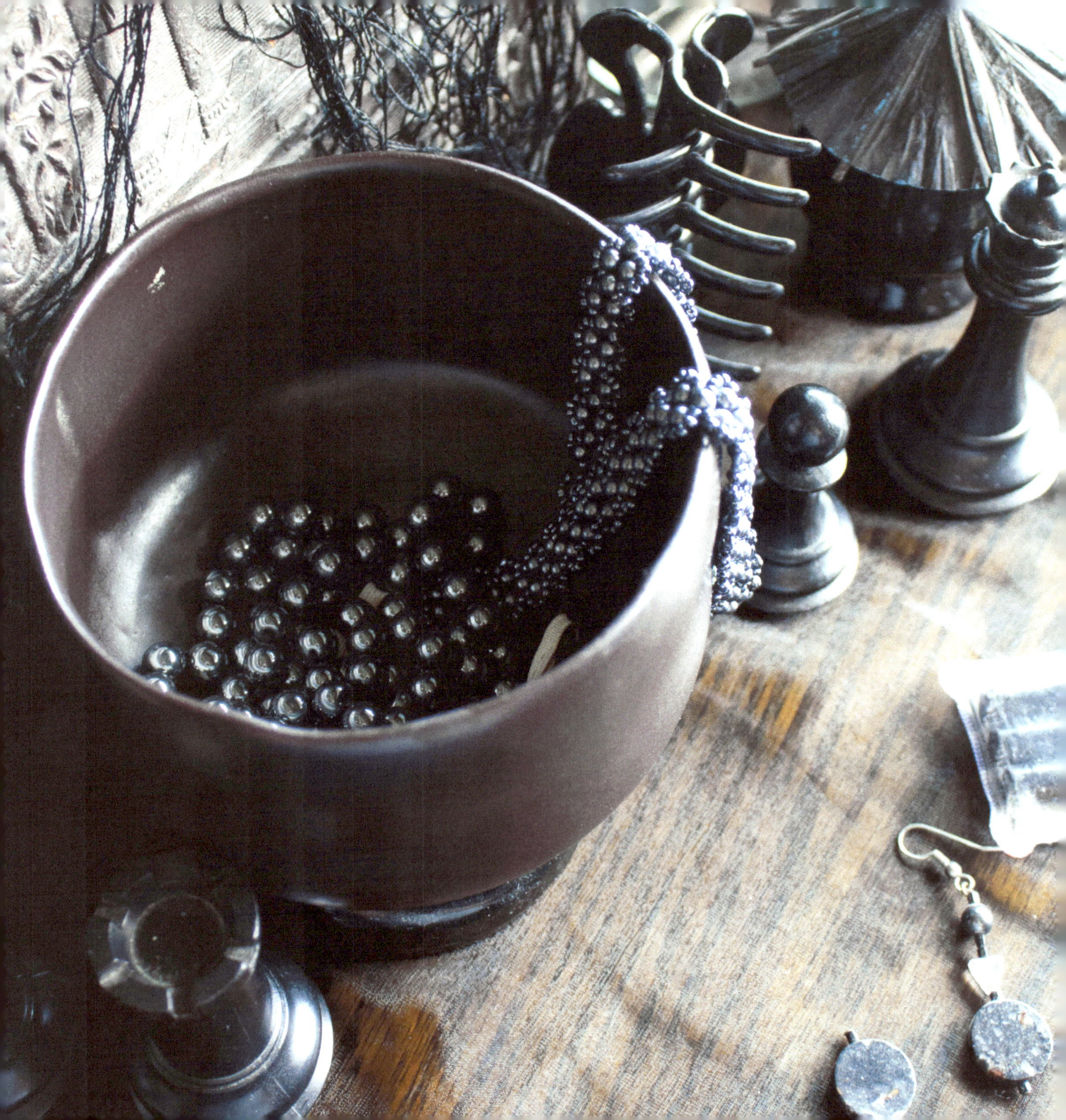

A DARK CHAMBER

The apartments were so irregularly disposed that the vision embraced but little more than one at a time. There was a sharp turn at the right and left, in the middle of each wall, a tall and narrow Gothic window looked out upon a closed corridor which pursued the windings of the suite. These windows were of stained glass whose color varied in accordance with the prevailing hue of the decorations of the chamber into which it opened. That at the eastern extremity was hung, for example, in blue—and vividly blue were its windows. The second chamber was purple in its ornaments and tapestries, and here the panes were purple. The third was green throughout, and so were the casements. The fourth was furnished and lighted with orange—the fifth with white—the sixth with violet. The seventh apartment was closely shrouded in black velvet tapestries that hung all over the ceiling and down the walls, falling in heavy folds upon a carpet of the same material and hue. But in this chamber only, the color of the windows failed to correspond with the decorations. The panes were scarlet—a deep blood color. Now in no one of any of the seven apartments was there any lamp or candelabrum, amid the profusion of golden ornaments that lay scattered to and fro and depended from the roof. There was no light of any kind emanating from lamp or candle within the suite of chambers. But in the corridors that followed the suite, there stood, opposite each window, a heavy tripod, bearing a brazier of fire, that projected its rays through the tinted glass and so glaringly lit the room… But in the western or black chamber the effect of the firelight that streamed upon the dark hangings through the bloodtinted panes was ghastly in the extreme, and produced so wild a look upon the countenances of those who entered, that there were few of the company bold enough to set foot within its precincts at all.

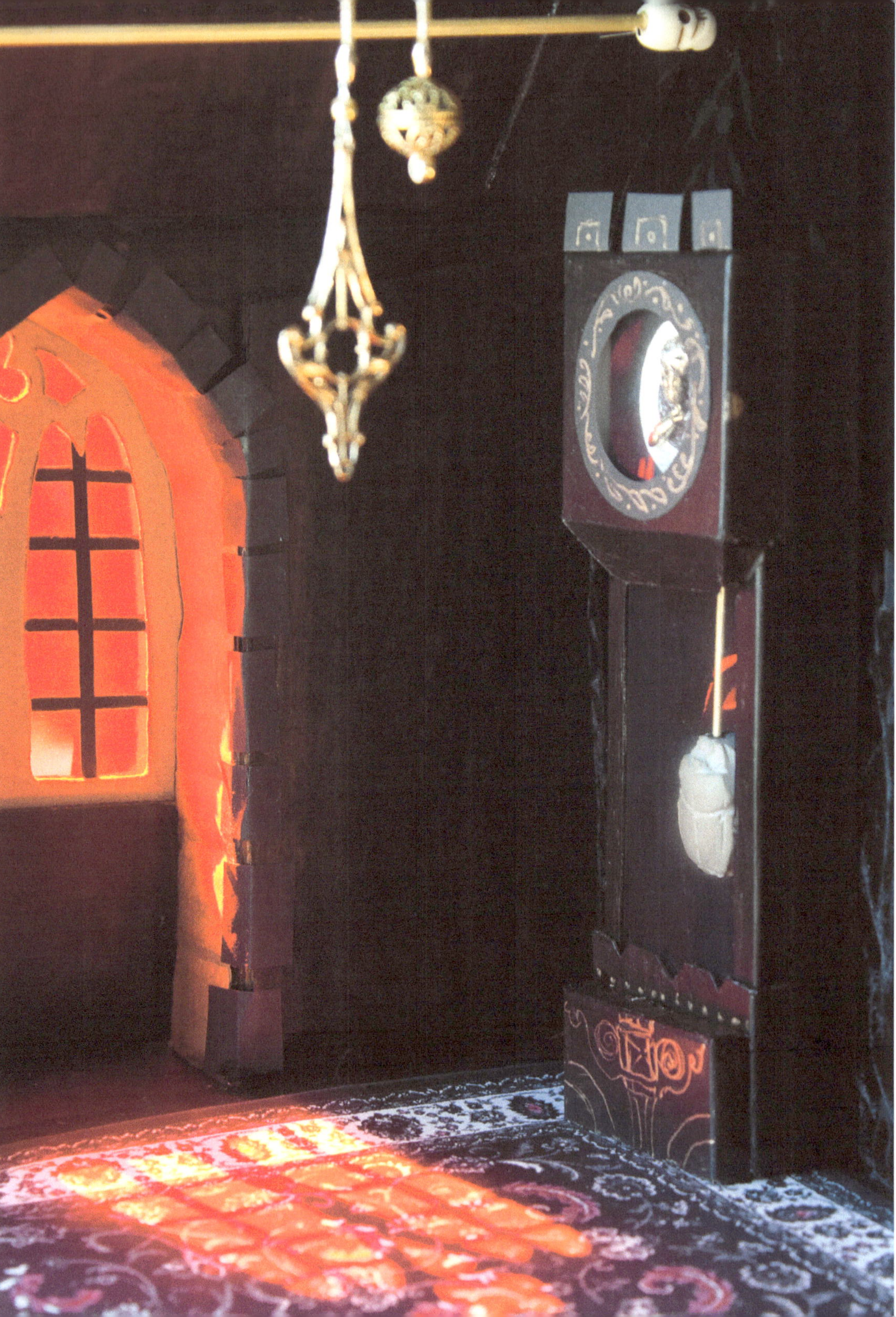

Again Kircher and his magic lantern. His illustration shows a chamber containing a hanging oil lamp. The flame is intensified by a concave mirror behind it, and then projected through a painting on glass set at a hole in the chamber wall. Later versions of this chamber were made of metal, with a little chimney on the top to vent the smoke and heat. Through the tube in the front they beamed their ghostly images onto the walls of dark rooms.[1] These images were often *of* ghosts, and people were sometimes fooled.

SYME'S BLACKS

Abraham Werner, 18th century German mineralogist, made what amounted to a color recipe book ("No. 17 Greyish Black, is composed of velvet black, with a portion of ash grey.") In one of the most poetic of assays into scientific order, Patrick Syme, a Scottish painter of wild flowers, extended this color index to include examples in the animal, vegetable, and mineral realms.[2] Each page of examples had a column of beautiful little hand-painted squares. Here is the text for the page of black squares:

17	Greyish Black	Water Ousel. Breast and upper Part of Back of Water Hen		Basalt
18	Bluish Black	Largest Black Slug	Crowberry	Black Cobalt Ochre
19	Greenish Black	Breast of Lapwing		Hornblende
20	Pitch or Brownish Black	Guillemot. Wing Coverts of Black Cock		Yenito Mica
21	Reddish Black	Spots on Large Wings of Tyger Moth. Breast of Pochard Duck	Berry of Fuschia Coccinea	Oliven Ore
22	Ink		Berry of Deadly Nightshade	Oliven Ore
23	Velvet Black	Mole. Tail Feathers of Black Cock	Black of Red and Black West-Indian Peas	Obsidian

Charles Darwin sailed on the Beagle with Syme's book in hand, and when he spoke of "a reddish-black vegetable mold," he was being as chromatically accurate as it was possible to be at the time.[3] But color is not that stable. It shifts from one animal to another. It shifts according to the quality and strength of light. Nor can we easily remember a specific shade, even one we see all the time.

■

As evidence that cultures differ in their very concept of color, Pastoureau cites the different Middle English terms for black: *swart* is matte black (frightening); *black* is 'luminous black' (like sable, luxurious, valuable).[4] "Black Is the Color of My True Love's Hair" sang Nina Simone to such devastating effect.

When I think of black, deep absolute black, I immediately summon textures—velvet, satin, wool, silk. Even to my mind's eye, the absence of sight invites in other senses. Black and classical music, its austerities. Matte finish of ebony fingerboard under the metal strings, the firefly depths of the lacquer on a grand piano, the curved threads of shine on a record as the needle lands. The light pools in rounded shapes on my black satin skirt, getting dressed for a high school orchestra performance, feeling itchy and insincere, insufficient practicing, panic, shame! abort, abort…

Moving on. Black is the fertile nadir of the cycle, rich and full of the rustling of pigment. In 1777, Buson described a stay at Kenshoji Temple in Miyazu, where he had become ill:

> *Once, about two o'clock in the morning, my fever being a little lower, I decided to go alone to the toilet and got up on my unsure feet. Leading to the toilet at the northwest corner of the building, there was a long hallway going beside that spacious room. With the lantern out, it was very dark. I opened the sliding door, and then, as I made the first step with my right foot, I stepped on something furry and round... I kicked out powerfully where I thought the thing was. But nothing at all touched me.*[5]

Buson infers that he was visited by a black masked *tanuki,* the magic badger-dog. Who knows where the night creatures come from or where they go.

And we must acknowledge, at the polar absolutes of black and white, that some of the possibilities are terrifying. Black plummets. I lose those I wish to keep and encounter those I would prefer to avoid. I have a boy here at the apartment for his tutoring session, and we're looking out the window. How often does *that* happen? he asks. For a dozen tornados line the horizon, and the sky is the black of oncoming apocalypse. All the time, I reassure him. No big deal. But we choose instead to settle in to our chess game next to the less frightening windows on the other side of the apartment, where we can watch the invasion of the nighttime town square by giant toy robots.

THE DREAM OF A NEW CURRENCY

My mother has been hired to design the new currency for the small country of B----. I am picking up the smooth black coins, distinguishable only by size. She used cobalt to make them, and in the process, discovered how the whole second half of the periodic table of elements is organized. I am wishing I could tell someone this, but who would believe me? The list of her accomplishments verges on the fantastic. (Cobalt? Basalt? But the coins look exactly like the steel burner crowns from our stove.)

Now the royal family of the small country has arrived for dinner, stiff in their formal garments that are so absolutely black, they have no visible seams. I didn't know they were coming, and I have nothing to feed them but baked black beans, which seems inadequate as a meal for royalty.

There are certain obvious things that first occurred to me when I started to write about color. I had thought to include a set of meals around each color (probably thinking in the background of Huysman's *À Rebour,* in which the narrator gives a decadent funeral feast of black food in mourning for his departed virility). I even made a few monochromatic meals, and some of them provided chance combinations of tastes that were not bad. But it seemed a little repetitive, in a project already full of lists and food.

LIKE ONE OF THE BLACK AMPHIBIANS OF MOUNT RORAIMA

A black frog, rubbery and sticky and sickly. I pick it up and hold its head under the spout of the water fountain so that it can drink. It clings to my finger with its boneless legs and powerful suction cups. I don't want to take care of it but I have to. With great bitterness, I throw it in a jar with some leaves and carry it around with me forever. Once awake, I know exactly who the frog is.

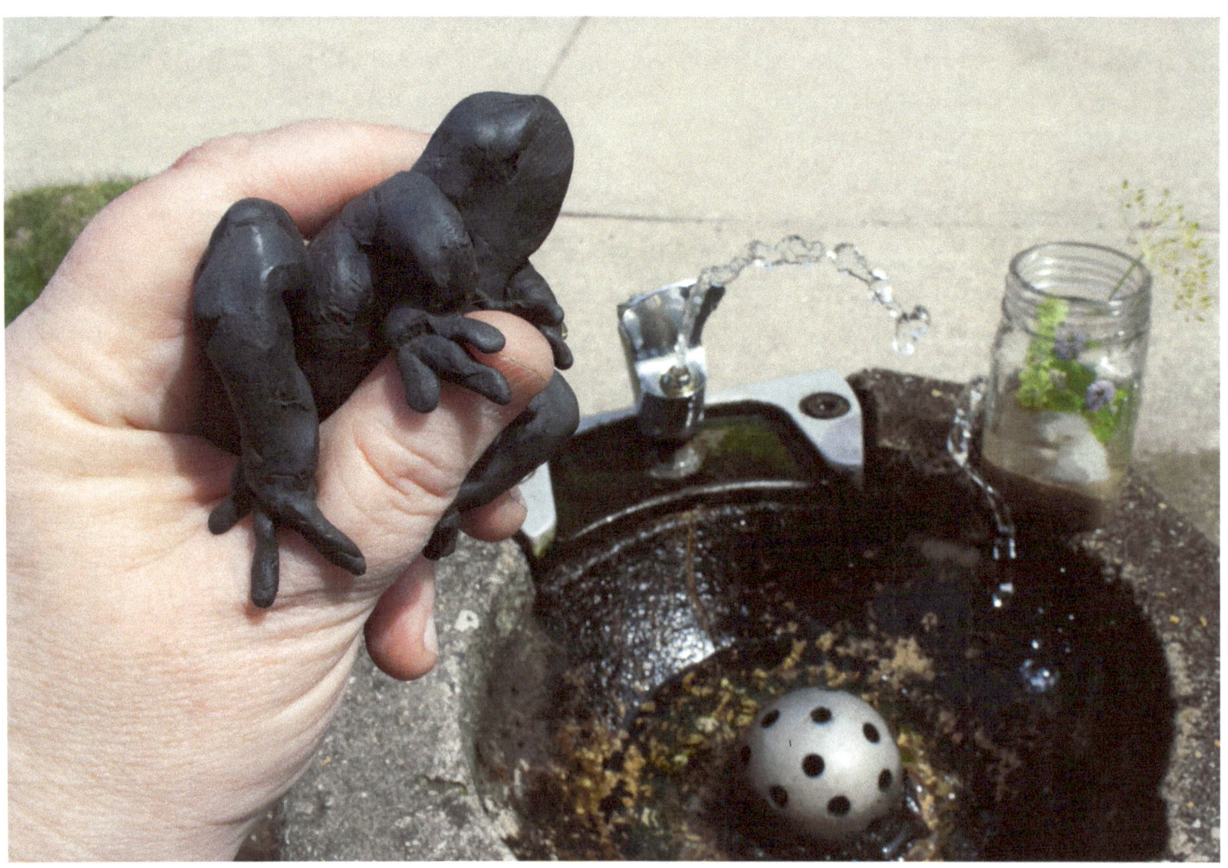

■

Our black cat Kali used to hide to sleep. We would call and call for her, and then see the green eyes, nothing else, looking out of the dark closet. Or see in the dark closet an even darker cat silhouette pulling darkness into itself. Or put a blind hand in and feel fur where we expected nothing. I should include a black page, to mirror the white one: the black page where our dead cat is. Because black is full of the surprise softness of fur and knives of teeth. The dark water is full of fish eating each other; the earth is full of bones and moles biting worms; owls hunt in the night sky.

And the blue-black swallows plummet and bank. The starlings land en masse and cover the maple tree with small movements and noise. *The voice of an evening crow announces the melancholy of autumn.*[6] Princess Crow, I used to call the cat when she cried.

BLACK COOKING SMELLS

Roasting coffee and the royal family at the door. All afternoon, the black beans have cooked in bourbon and pomegranate molasses, to be served with forbidden rice and huitlacoche, a very dark wine, and black cherries in a reduction of balsamic vinegar. Or so they would have done were I including monochromatic meals. A few black beans, though, mixed with coffee beans, are scattered among the go stones.

■

Vine black, one of the oldest and best of all black pigments, an early ingredient for ink, is made from the charcoal of grape vines. The dense wood burns down to a relatively pure concentration of carbon. And the ink branches leach into the pale sky.

> What do you think of the beans? Are They Good?
>
> I'm not really sure how to answer when you talk like that, said Bobby. It's a double parody of a question.

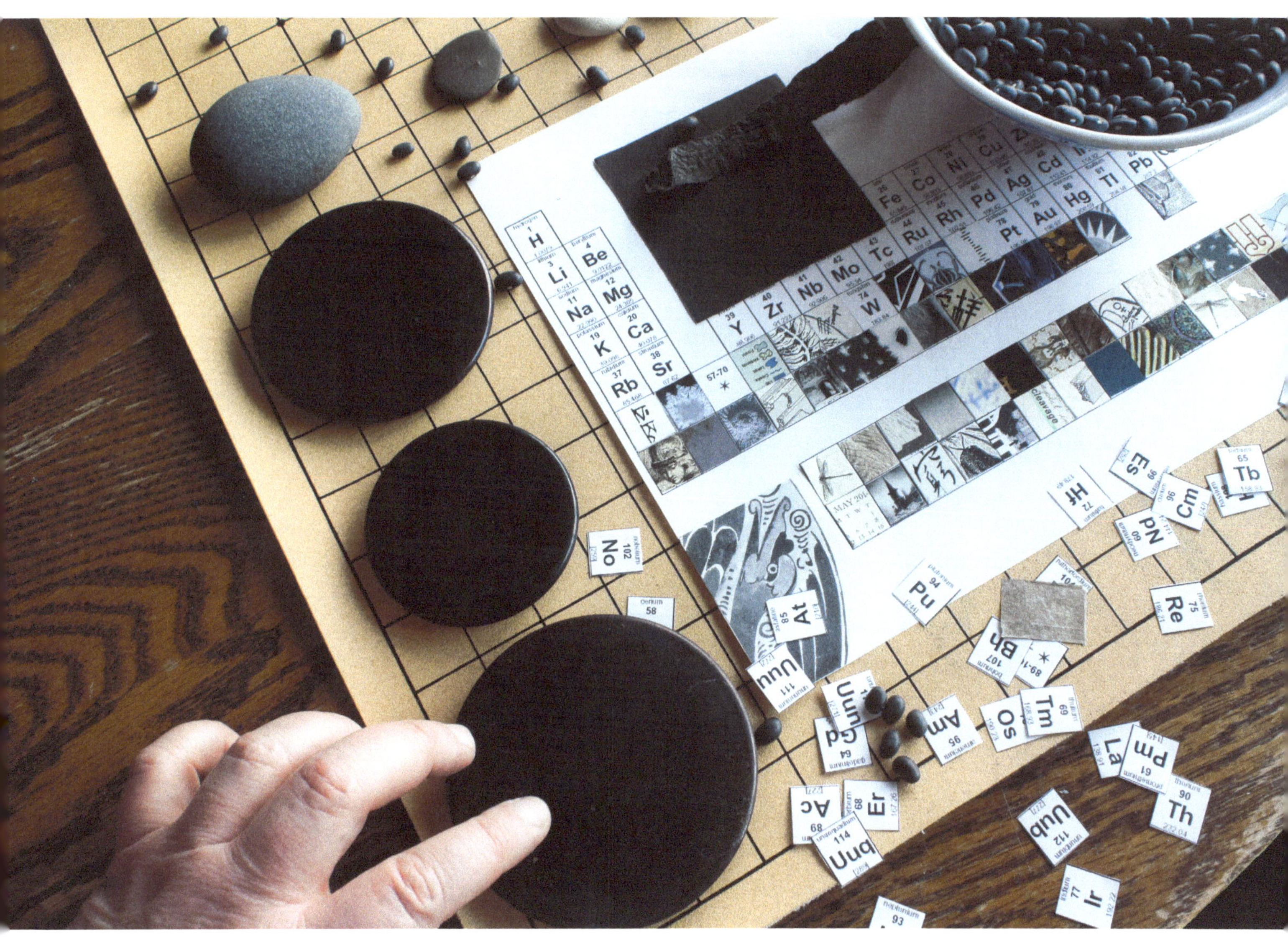

AN IRON CASING, AN IRON INK

Like one of the black amphibians of Mount Roraima, a table mountain topped by black stones eroded into formations more ridiculous than any Road Runner cartoon.

When we biked west out of Paris toward Brittany, we got to register the way the local stone erupted into architecture. The leaf carved limestone of the Loire Valley became crude granite too hard to carve details into, then sheets of slate too frangible to carve at all. Angers was made foreboding by its ruined fortress high on top of its slate outcrop (and the swallows circled overhead). Slate is the material traditionally used for black go stones.

■

White plum blossoms: in the embassy, the fragrance of ink.[7] Beside vine black, foundations for ink included bone char, ivory char, and lamp black. I was reading an article on the latest theory decoding the Voynich Manuscript and, I swear, not thinking about Athanasius Kircher at all, but he Is Ubiquitous. Georgius Barschius wrote from Prague in 1639 to tell Kircher in Rome about a book Barschius owned, "a mysterious book that was written in an unknown script and that was profusely illustrated with pictures of plants, stars and chemical secrets." The brownish-black ink used in the Voynich manuscript has been analyzed to contain "iron, sulfur, calcium, potassium, and carbon"—probably an iron gall ink.[8]

When adapting ink for the printing press, adding iron to bone char or vine black helped the words to bite permanently into the white paper. All those little serif teeth. And the flood of printing, metal type coated with metal-enriched ink before marking bleached paper in repetition after repetition, rose alongside the accreting crystalline structures of manufacture (and their accompanying erratic plumes of poisonous effluvia).

My aunt once cried with chagrin that the family telephone was black. For my grandparents, black was the color of the very edge of technological advancement, allowable within the ethic and aesthetic of Protestant sobriety[9]; for my aunt at fourteen, telephones were now a test of fashion sense, and her parents had not passed it, so she had not passed it, and everything was ruined.

■

Kircher had great faith in the "didactic image." Over and over he committed to inked engraving and white page the figure of the scarab man, a beetle with the head of Horus, copied from the margins of an ancient Egyptian tablet. He thought it the key to the ancient Egyptian world view. Above the scarab was a winged sphere ribboned with a snake. The scarab held a tablet with writing, his head was crowned with the crescent moon, and on his shoulder was a spiral. Kircher decoded each element of this picture with a mixture of erudition, intuition, and willful blindness. The beetle that pushes a ball of dung before it was earth's "moderator or motive power." The spiral was the circular paths of the planets. The sphere was the "'soul of the world' infusing life into things." Horus was the sun; the moon the moon (my personal favorite). Within its crescent was a small cross with a point for each element of the material plane. The tablet spelled out the Greek word for *philo,* 'love,' although no one else could see the same letters on it that Kircher did.[10]

■

I never in all my life felt so uncomfortable or—I may as well at once confess it—so frightened. There, in that empty hull, over that boardless floor, over these rotting joists, somebody or something was dragging some heavy weight. What, I could not imagine; only the shrieks, the blows, the groans, the dull thumping sounds, compelled me to suspect the worst,—to feel convinced that I was actually within some few feet of a horrible murder then being committed. I could form no idea of who the victim was, or who was the assassin. That I actually heard the sounds I had no doubt; that they were growing louder and more distinct I felt painfully aware. The horror of the situation was intense. If only I could strike a light, and see what was passing close there—but I had no matches. I could hear a sound as of some one breathing

> *slowly, stertorously, then a dull groan. And once more the cruel sodden blows fell again, followed by a drip, drip, and heavy drop in the dank water below, from which the sickening smell rose, pungent, reeking, horrible.*
>
> *The dragging shuffling noise now began again. It came quite close to me, so close that I felt I had only to put out my hand to touch the thing.*

In my favorite ghost story, the narrator has gotten stranded on a beached ship and taken shelter for the night in the empty metal hold. In his terror, he will leave his shelf and fall into the stinking water below and have to find his way out, with no light, as those sounds (the only terror the story contains) play in a continuous loop. Black is as crowded as the market is full of phantoms.

> *World exhibitions thus provide access to a phantasmagoria which a person enters in order to be distracted… a balcony of cast iron would represent the ring of Saturn, and people who venture out on it would find themselves carried away in a phantasmagoria where they seem to have been transformed into inhabitants of Saturn.*[11]

(I tend to read Walter Benjamin with reverence but without much understanding, just as some people once opened the Bible at random for prophetic guidance. What *is* a dialectical image? The past and present connect, something something, boom! Combustion occurs…)

(Phantasmagoria: my mind always goes to Edward Gorey, and his charming inked morbidities.)

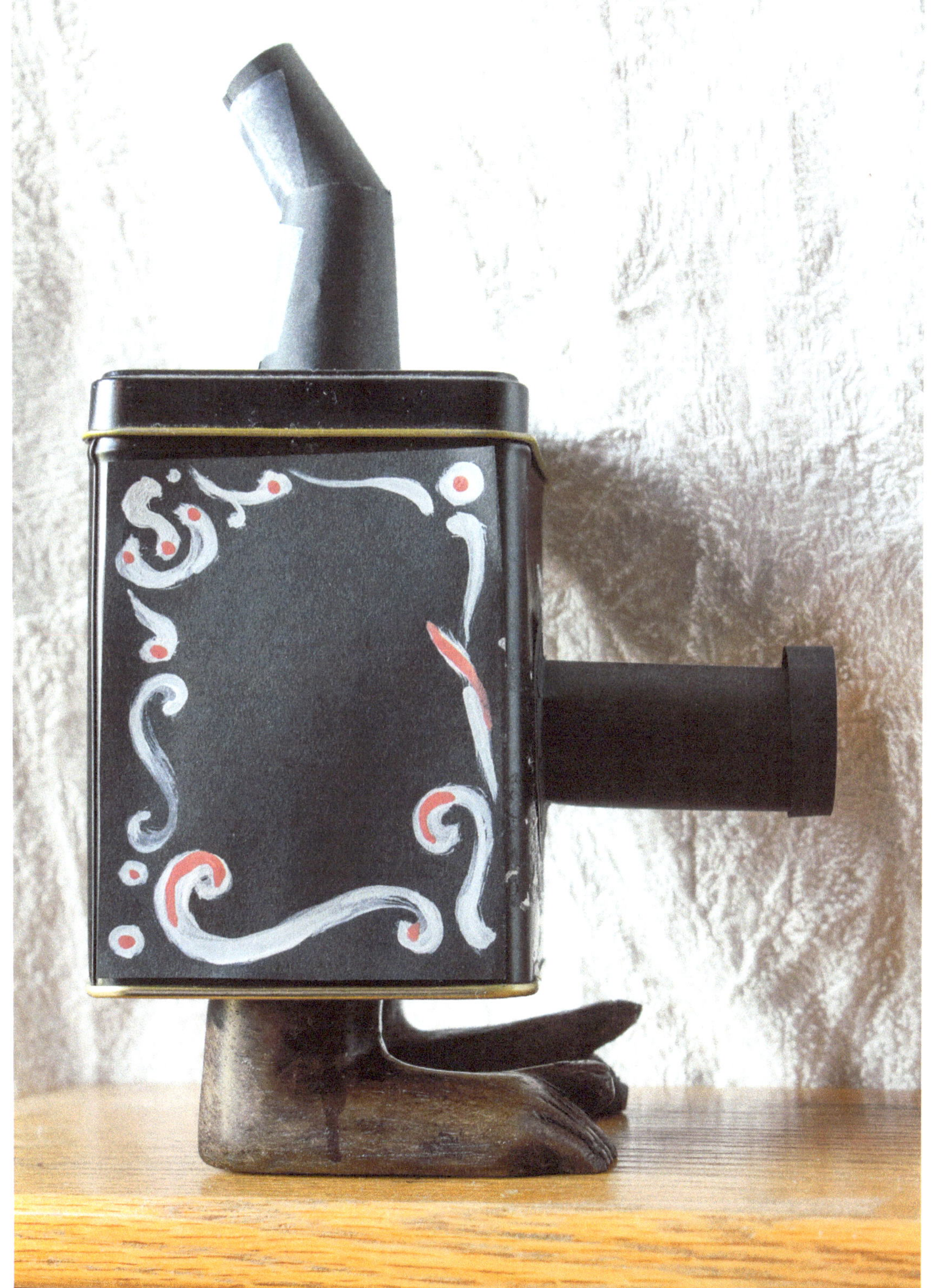

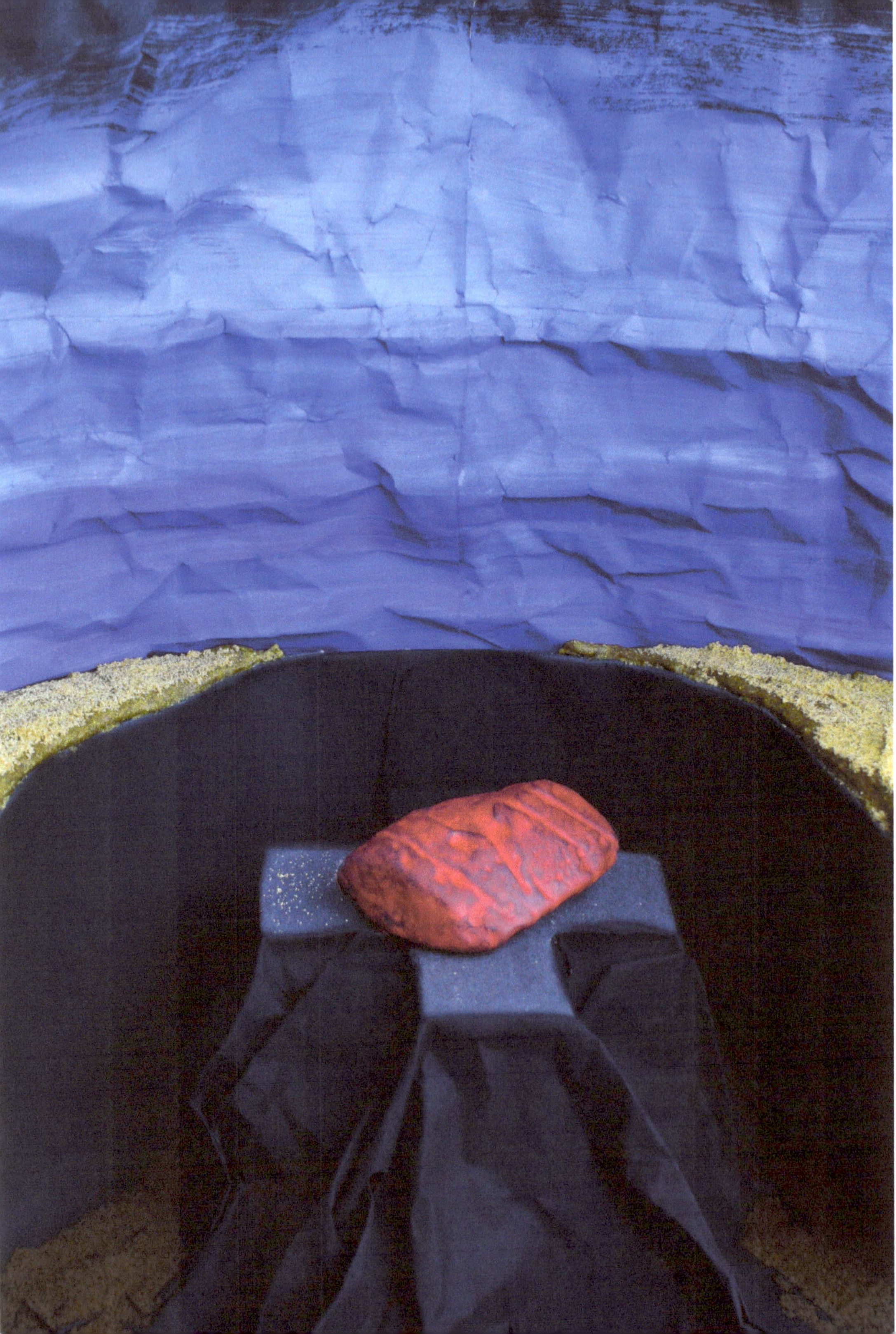

White and black, red yellow and blue: now we have a world, a language. A symbolic order, Pastoureau would say. As in all my dreams about archeology, we are digging to create the archeology site we know should be there. Digging a cross-shaped floor surrounded by a pit, all under the rocky dome walled in night blue. In the center of the cross is a large outcrop of rock we are painting fire red. The sandy floor is yellow for earth; we are paving the surface of the cross with a mixture of coal tar and gun powder that adheres terribly to our hands.

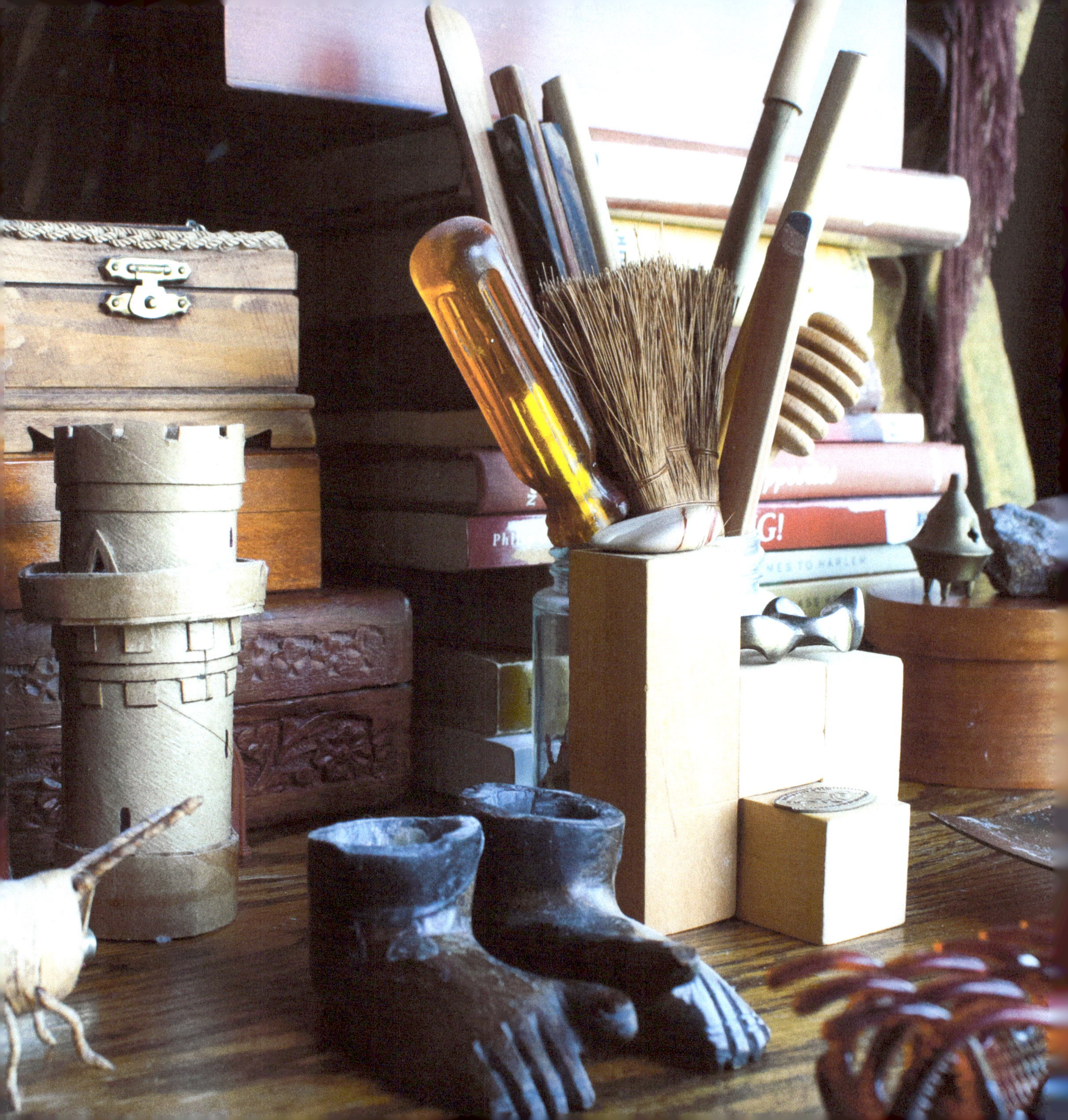

THE BEAUTIFUL MELANCHOLY OF CARDBOARD

Nicolai Fechin, Russian architect in Taos, designed his house to integrate the local adobe architecture with the folk carvings of Russia, also the occasional Asian element, like the bell shaped windows in the smoking room. The house flamboyantly exaggerates its quiet, old-fashioned materials, smooth clay and roughly carved wood and ornate wrought iron, so that there are many worked surfaces upon which the soul may adhere. Fechin first worked out the design roughly in cardboard; his estate still has the model. The effort to see into the rooms of this cardboard house, to peer past the visible sine wave of corrugation where the windows are cut into the white gouached walls, fills me with a lovely sadness and a desire for imitation.

CONTEMPLATION IN A TEA GARDEN

The traditional Japanese store of color terms is a miracle of evocative specificity. Brown is *cha-iro,* 'tea color' (after green tea, but even green tea brewed in the cup looks more brown than green.) Some varieties of browns (or at least they look brown to my eye) include:

> *Sabitetsuonando:* 'rusted iron storeroom'
> *Namakabe iro:* 'fresh, undried wall color'
> *Kobicha:* 'flattery tea,' 'flirtatious tea'

■

The author names few colors in "Childe Roland to the Dark Tower Came," mostly black and grey, but in this poem out of all his poems, his name stains the dull colors to brown, like tea on old paper. Brown is the color of craft and its dissolution, and all nostalgia, even for awfulness. World War One: the brown war. *I guess'd what skull-like laugh would break, what crutch 'gin write my epitaph for pasttime in the dusty thoroughfare…*

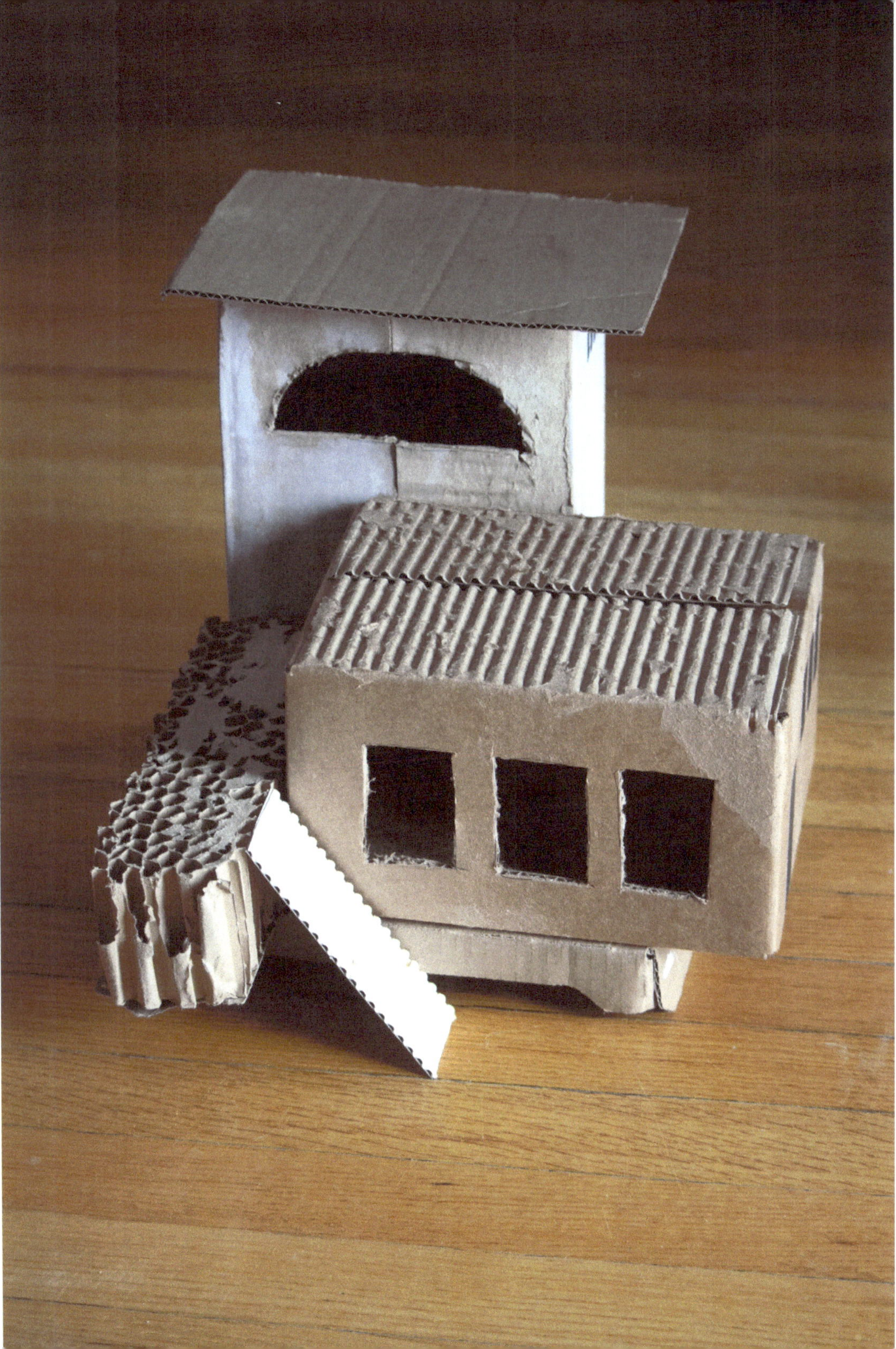

CLOVE TEA IN TAOS

I am visiting the elderly academic and her brother in their living room filled with carved oak and the perfume of old books. The professor is making me some kind of magic tea that is supposed to heal all my particular ills or tell my fortune or something, and I am humoring her. *Chōjicha,* 'clove tea,' *kyaya-iro,* 'aloeswood color'—she keeps adding more spices, anise, cinnamon, cloves, to a little brown pottery bowl with a wide lip, and grinding them up with a pestle. This is going to be more of an undrinkable paste than a tea. She asks have I ever tried this before, and I say one time, in Taos. But then I remember another time I tried magic tea, and then another, and another—I have no grounds for criticizing her, do I?

As part of the tea ritual, she tells me that I should make sure there are no weapons in the house. This seems discourteous to her brother, considering how he is going to die, but he doesn't act offended. I naturally start with the many desks in his study. Drawer after drawer, no guns, no knives, no ninja throwing stars, but one drawer is full of odd green fruits or pods. I take one back to the living room to ask what it is. As I come back into the room

THE ELABORATING SERPENT

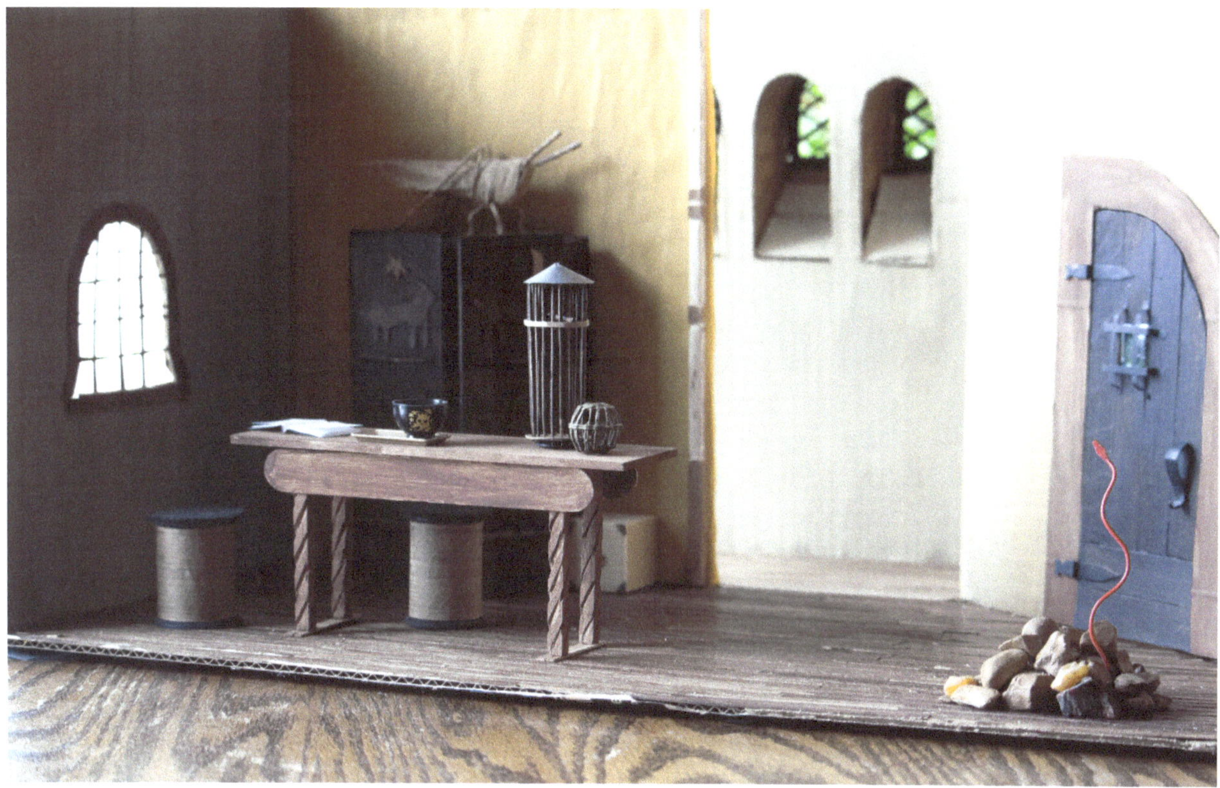

I happen to glance at the pile of rocks in the corner. A little string is rising up, right there, no, a red-brown ribbon, Snake! I say, tripping slightly and pointing. It has spotted a tiny spider on a thread and has climbed the air with delicately opened jaw to eat it. As I look, it grows bigger; now it's the size of a garter snake, now a king snake, and more detailed, as if my looking gives it fuller existence. The brother goes over and gives its huge red-brown coils a cautious nudge; it now has various dragonish crests and knobs. Aren't you going to kill it? I ask. Or at least grab it and take it out before it gets too big. No she says, that will just get its slime all over us (snakes are *not* slimy). Her brother does manage to gently herd the creature which is his death out the door, and we go on as if nothing has happened.

I am lying in bed, asleep, and as I wake up, I catch a wooden chair crawling across the ceiling. Not only is it walking, it is bending and flattening itself so slyly, like the little cockroach it is. I shout, Chair! and it straightens out immediately and clatters on the floor. But we both know its secret is out. I then notice other inanimate objects deforming themselves, out of the corner of my eye, when they think I'm not looking. My relationship to furniture will never be the same.

Julia Prewit Brown, following Benjamin, discusses the bourgeois interior as phantasmagoria.[1] The objects of middle class comfort seem to us to appear out of thin air, to derive to us naturally, not as the recipient of someone's labor, but by decree of the universe. We fill our domestic spaces with souvenirs from the far reaches of empire, rare exported materials to show our wealth and sophistication, the most natural and God-given expression of our true selves, ignoring the accompanying ghosts of violence and suffering that procured these spoils for us. (And you know *on this sofa the aunt cannot but be murdered*. But eventually time turns violence, like bloodstains, to a mellowed brown.)[2]

Uguisu-cha: 'nightingale tea.' *Hiwa-cha:* 'finch tea.' *Benikeshinezumi:* 'red vanishing mouse.'

I visit my office after a long break. While I have been away, a brown bird has become trapped there. I see that someone left a dish of calamine lotion for it, but the dish is now dry and empty. I pour some water in my palm, and the bird drinks weakly with its rough bill. As I lift it carefully to carry it to the bathroom for a proper drink from the faucet, I see its mate lying dead on the table, even more wasted away to string. But then, as I walk past, it stirs, alive after all. I didn't know they were in my office, I swear, but still, this new nightmare of failing to take proper care of something weak in my charge is vivid and horrifying.

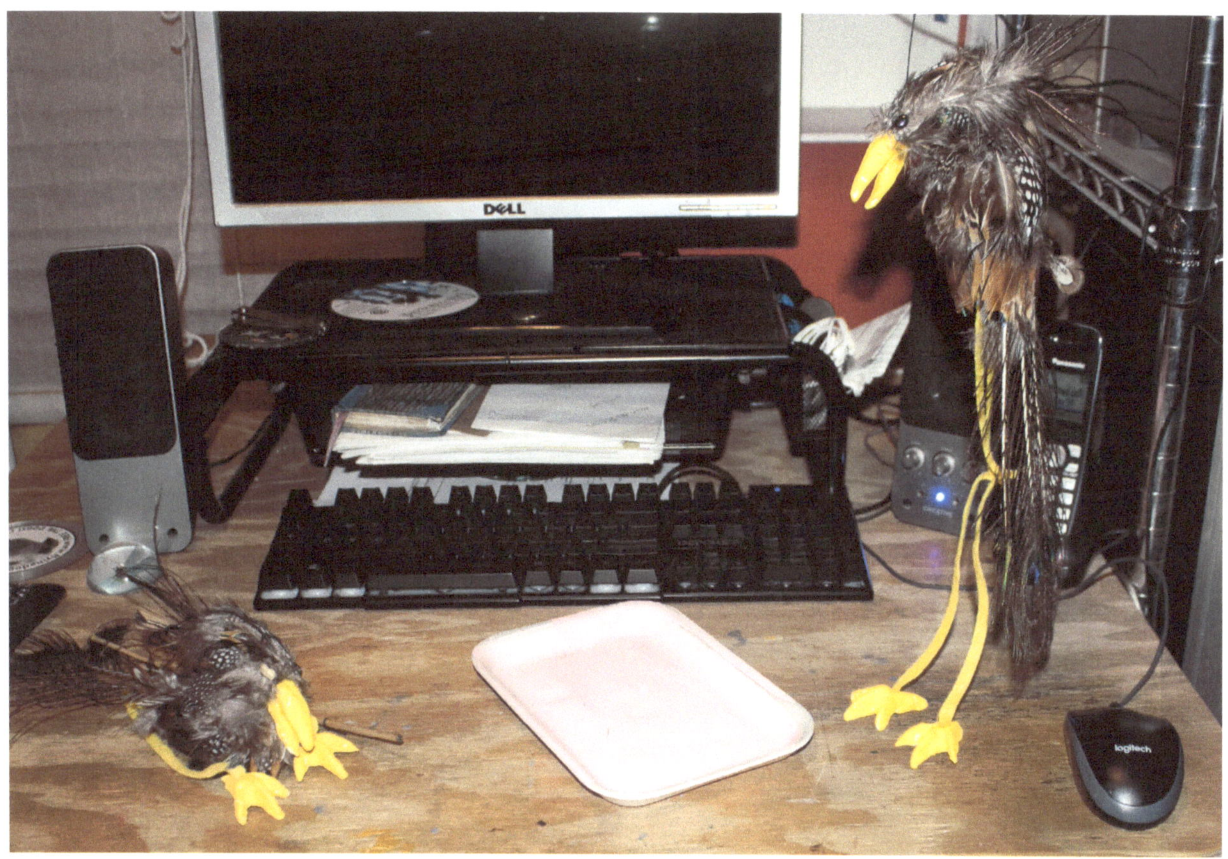

As Europe emptied Egypt of its mummies, carting them off to museums, or grinding them up for fertilizer, one of the oddest uses it found for them was for pigment. The brown was mostly a product of the bitumen used in embalming, but embalming methods were not uniform over time, so the paint varied considerably in shade and opacity. When the painter Edward Burne-Jones found out what poor dead fellow human beings were in his paint, he is said to have had an impromptu funeral and interred his paint tubes in the ground.[3]

And the sparrows made noises in the leafless branches. Small things in our care. *Bush warbler, what are you doing? rustling away in the frost-covered bush.*[4]

■

I am in the process of constructing a life sized model of the front half of a horse. When it gets attached to the wall, it needs to be connected to the ventilation, of course, or the stuffing will mildew. But on examination, I fear our little cabin on stilts lacks any sort of ventilation system. And how it shakes in the constant earthquakes. I doubt it will even remain standing much longer.

DEATH BY OPIUM CAKE

Kaba-iro: 'birch color.' *Susutake-iro:* 'sooty bamboo color.' *Mirucha:* 'sea pine tea.' *Ainezumi:* 'indigo mouse.' *Rikyūcha:* 'Rikyū's tea,' Rikyū being the 16th century master of tea ceremony. Your

tea

my

dear.

Kircher:

> *It certainly is very strong. Unless I had learned to drink it at the frequent invitations by our father, I could hardly have been induced to believe it. It is a diuretic and marvellously opens the bladder. It frees the head from vapours. Nature has not given literary men a more noble and apt remedy for helping them do a great amount of work during long vigils. Although at first it is weak and bitter, after a while it becomes pleasant and one develops such an appetite that he can scarcely abstain from it. Although Turkish coffee and Mexican chocolate have the same effect, tea is better, for it is more temperate. Chocolate heats one up too much when the weather is warm, and coffee makes the bile ascend. Tea is always harmless and it is marvellously effective not once, but even a hundred times a day.*[5]

Kircher was the collector and keeper of his own Museum Kircherianum in Rome, or rather, something between a cabinet of curiosities and a museum. Rome was the center of a vast gathering of curiosities from the saved or soon to be saved reaches of the world, and Kircher's galleries housed hitherto undreamed of natural wonders, animal and plant specimens…

A tea bag thrown away. Buson wrote that one courts poetic inspiration by enjoying the company of authors from past ages. I like to think of these as brown ghosts.

Seek out Kikaku, visit Ransetsu, recite Sodō, and accompany Onitsura. Meet those four elders every day. Go far away from the marketplace, stroll among the trees in the garden, hold a banquet by a mountain stream, and enjoy a conversation over saké wine.[6]

■

I'm in rather bad health, live in a hole that's lost somewhere between calcinated tree stumps and, periodically, a sort of parabolic shell dawdles by and coughs... The tobacco shop is both fat and brunette; I'm even beginning to smell British (shoe polish, tea, and blond tobacco) and dance the waltz of vampires—while drinking tea with milk—nostalgic things that died before the war... (But cockle, spurge, according to their law might propagate their kind, with none to awe, and as for the grass, it grew as scant as hair in leprosy; thin dry blades prick'd the mud...) Several times I've told a colonel to whom I'm attached that I'll push a bit of wood into his earens. In an ex-village, a very narrow pigsty hung with blankets, I dress in khaki and fight the Germans. Then I take a theory for troubling paintings for a walk around villages in ruins...[7]

Actually it's unclear if death was the intended destination when Jacques Vaché took to a Nantes hotel room to smoke and ingest opium on this day in 1919 with four companions (one of whom also died). Certainly Vaché's disdainful detachment from everyone and everything made self-destruction a plausible possibility; his world-weariness and cynicism were so all-consuming that it's almost immaterial whether he *meant* to overdose or not.

I do not think I want his troubling presence among my brown ghosts. *A thrown-away tea bag among the fallen leaves.*[8] But while I am not so haunted by Vaché or Breton, I am somewhat haunted by Breton's haunting by Vaché, by his letters. "But then what would Vaché be, without his letters? Only a series of fragments and anecdotes. A ghost of a ghost."[9]

Many conversations with Bobby end with my saying, No, you can't have any opium.

Can I put our opium conversations in the book?

If you want to. Why would you want to? Where would they go?

In the opium section.

Why (with growing suspicion) is there an opium section?

Opium cake is the only brown poison I can think of.

That is a terrible oversimplification.

Here we go. Whatever you say next is *so* going into the book.

Think about how long it was the only cure for pain and suffering that people had. I was just reading about Homer's use of the term *nepenthe.* A medicine for sorrow. A cure for memory. Some people argue that it must have been based on opium.

The Homeric cure for memory. Captured and sequestered. And his criticism is fair; many of the things I have listed as poisonous have medicinal benefits in smaller quantities. On the other hand, some are poisonous in any quantity and have been used medicinally anyway. And yes, the day may come when he or I require vast quantities of opium in some form or other. But for now, in conclusion:

No you can't have any opium.

TO THE DARK TOWER CAME

Those are terrible times when the weather is the same color as the ground. The dust storm on the horizon like a great cat's paws clamping down on a mouse. In March of 2008 in San Antionio, for a few moments it rained mud, and *in the midst… the Tower itself. The round squat turret, blind as the fool's heart, built of brown stone, without a counterpart in the whole world.* Its galleries housed rare wonders, Egyptian obelisks, optical and magnetic instruments. The museum was faithful to a kind of order, a mirror of Kircher's mind. Bacon and Descartes had already begun to establish the rudiments of the scientific method, but for Kircher, experiements were done to confirm the already known-to-be-true. "There was no skepticism or nominalism about Kircher, who assumed that since everything in the universe was connected, it was all knowable if only one had a framework into which to fit it."[10]

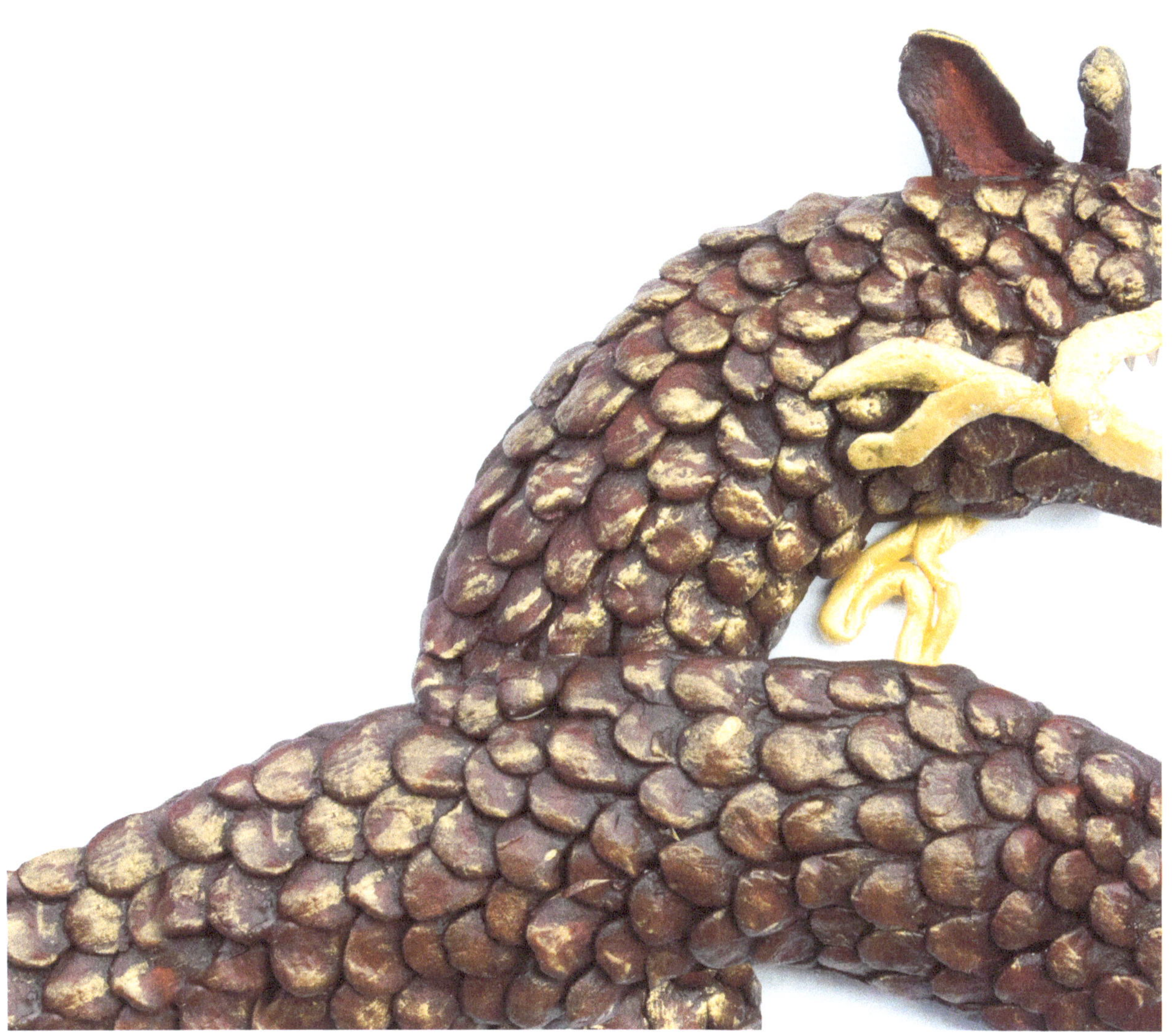

Aku-iro: 'lye colored.' *Testuonando:* 'iron storage.' *Sabi-iro:* the rust color of old roller skates. The pile of rocks where the snake lives are *tonocha:* 'polished tea.'

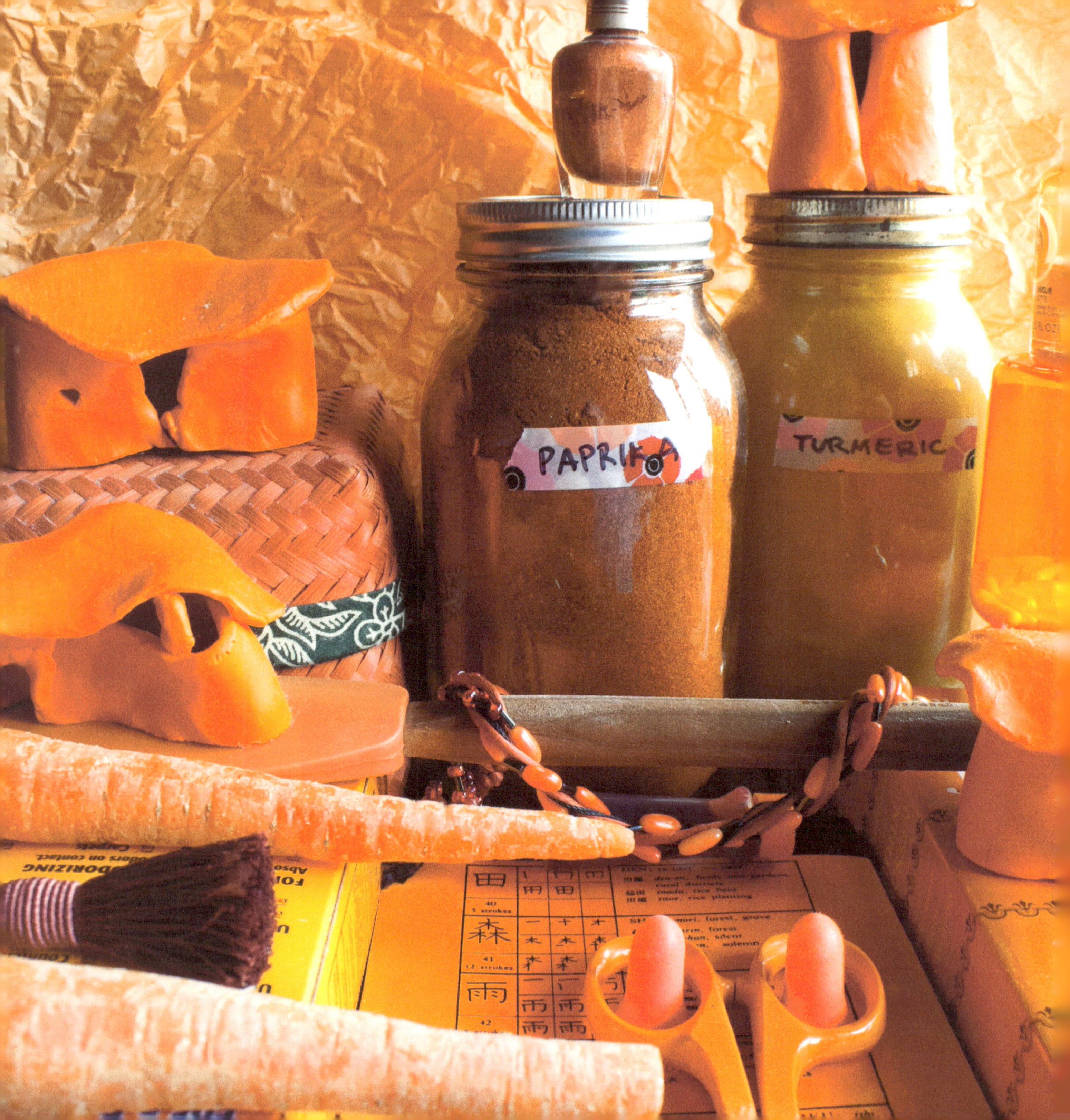
TURMERIC

A DECAYED HOUSE

Yet you are not to imagine, that the Fires and Waters, &c. are really thus disposed in Nature underground. For whoever has seen them? But this only was to signifie, according to the best imagination of the Author, that they are after some well-ordered and artificial, or organiz'd way or other, contriv'd by Nature; and that the Under-ground World is a well fram'd House, with distinct Rooms, Cellars, and Store-houses, by great Art and Wisdom fitted together; and not, as many think, a confused and jumbled heap or Chaos of things, as it were, of Stones, Bricks, Wood, and other Materials, as the rubbish of a decayed House, or an House not yet made.[1]

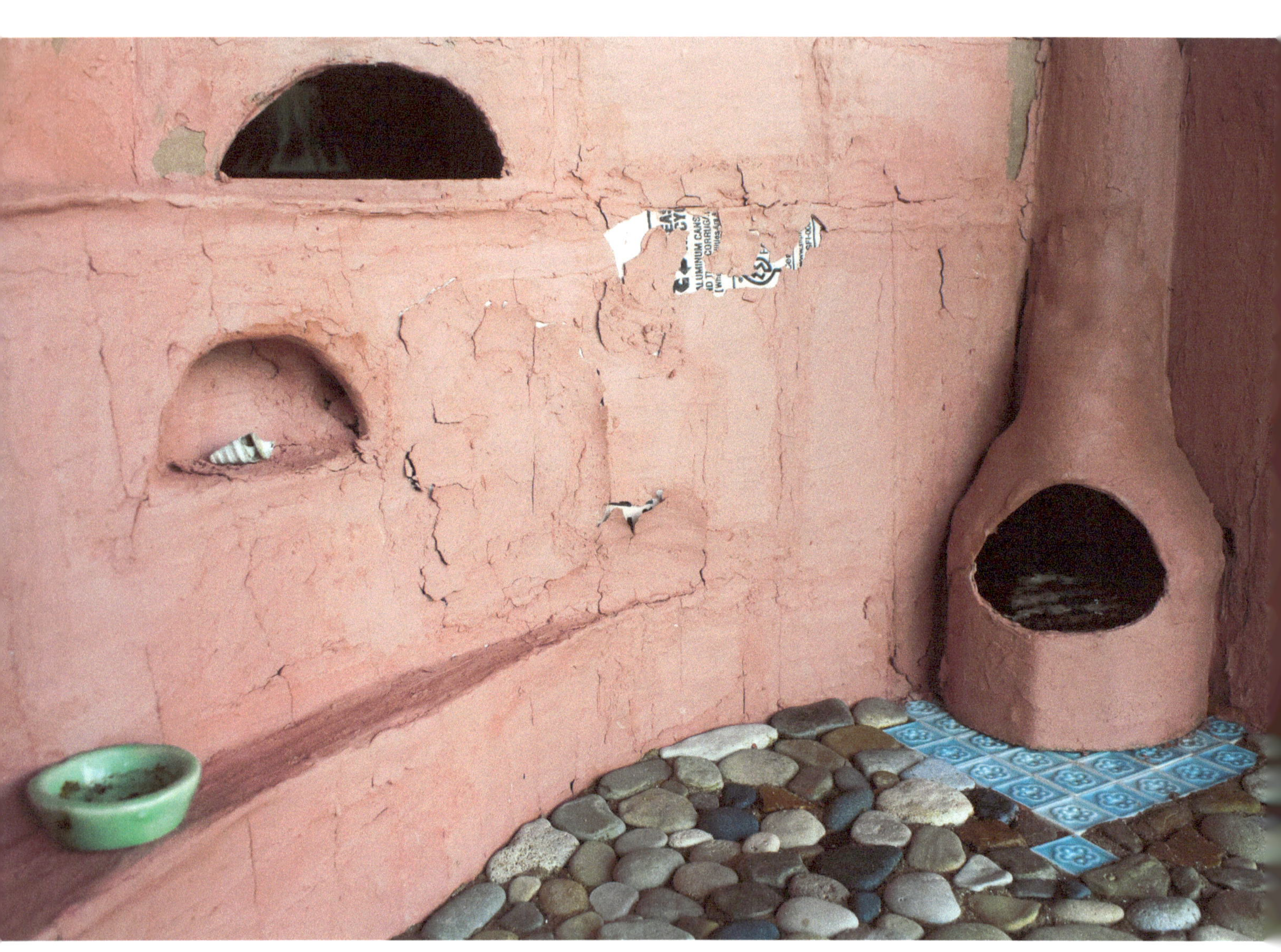

RIPE FRUIT FIRE

Hearth fire and apocalypse. In the great chain of being, Kircher showed, the fiery dry constellation of Aries corresponds to the head and four descending groups of plants, all to be used to treat the head's ailments.[2]

Orange is the only English basic color term that is named after something. Before oranges were imported, we did not name this color. Orange things were red (like foxes) or golden. Even oranges were at first called in English 'golden apples.' If you really needed to specify orange, you could say, as Chaucer did, that something was *betwixt yelow and reed*—the very awkwardness of the construction a sign of its rarity.[3] Ironic, since so many fruits are orange, and ripe fruit is one of the things our vision is for. Aristotle believed we see by shooting fire out of our eyeballs. Yes, it sounded more elegant when he said it, but that is basically what he said. Let us pause for a moment and enjoy the B movie visuals that invokes.

> Aristotle tells us that Empedocles... likened the eye to a lantern, "a gleam of fire blazing through the stormy night, adjusting thereto... the transparent sides, which scatter the breath of the winds... while, out through them leaping the fire." Just so, "the primeval fire, fenced within the membranes and delicate tissues [of the eye] fended off the deep surrounding flood, while letting through the fire" that makes the surroundings visible.[4]

Color and empire. What they saw they took. Tyrian purple, alabaster, gold, cinnabar, lapis, ivory char, mummy, cochineal, indigo, coffee, paprika, tea, malachite, orpiment... Each pigment stains its own webbed overlay of lines of extraction, forced labor, naked domination and trade. It's worse than the anatomist's layered plates of nerves and veins, worse than the subway map of Tokyo. Medieval European towns forced dyers and their smelly workshops to the edge of town and treated them like pariahs, no matter how beloved their products were. 17th century Spanish illustrations show the Spanish and natives of "New Spain" tending cochineal plantations together, but in fact the labor was almost all native, the oversight Spanish.[5] Working in the lapis lazuli mines of Afghanistan without masks destroys the miners' lungs; war disrupts the export of the stones and leaves them without a living.[6] As peasant farmers starved, Louis XIV decreed that oranges should ripen for the court's delectation in the trees of the hothouse orangerie of Versailles. Indigo dye may not have been poisonous, but the process of making it was noxious in the extreme. Slaves in pre-revolutionary Georgia who had to work bent over vats to agitate the rotting plants, breathing in the fumes, are reported to have died after an average of five to seven years.[7] Kastan describes how 18th century French soldiers fighting the slave rebellion on Sainte Domingue wore blue uniforms that might have been dyed with indigo grown by the very slaves they were fighting. He adds, "The dispiriting history of the indigo trade is… an irresistible reminder that Newton's immaterial color was actually an all-too-material dye and that its commercial production was always dependent upon coercive structures of power."[8]

A DREAM OF CHAMPIONS

Many volcanos have started to smoke. We are all very nervous. The slope is now covered with emerging kiln-lit funnels, fumaroles, cones, towers, and the streams of ash flow up into the night sky to form clouds of smoke, their bellies colored by fire. But beyond the slope glow the lights of the stadium. It is the night of the male championship, and they will not call off the game. We stand by, keeping watch, hearing occasional updates on the score, ready to force the men to evacuate when the eruptions begin. *Which shall at length come to pass, in that fulness of time, when all the Reins of unruly Nature shall be broke loose, and the Cataracts, or Flood-gates as it were, of subterraneous fire flung open; by the command of the Divine Power, not only the Earth, but even the Elements shall melt with fervent heat, to the ruine and destruction of the whole World*. Who's winning? I (don't care, I really don't care, but still)

find myself asking.

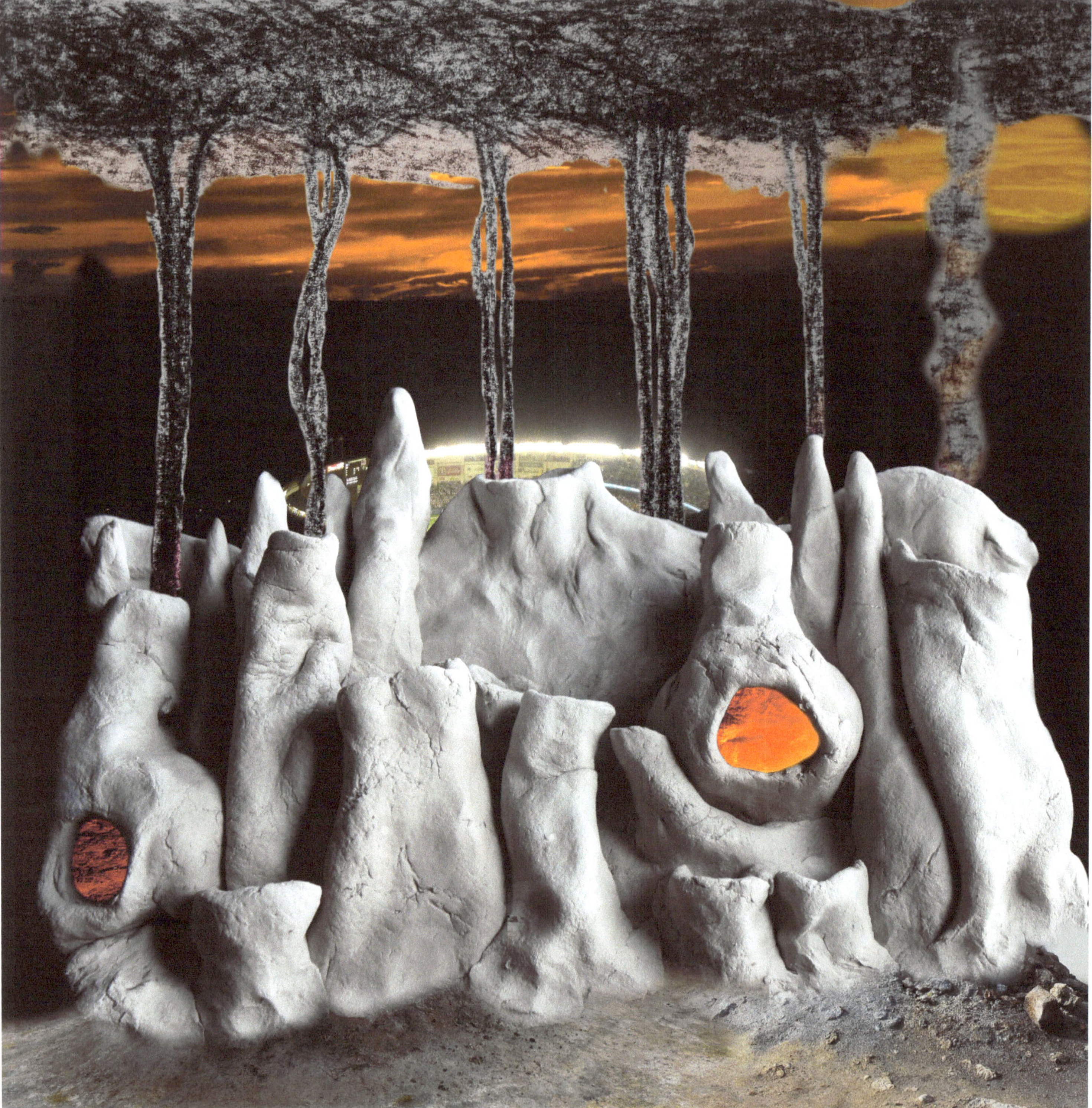

ANIMALS WHO ARE ON FIRE

In what distant deeps or skies
Burnt the fire of thine eyes?
On what wings dare he aspire?
What the hand, dare seize the fire?

And what shoulder, & what art,
Could twist the sinews of thy heart?
And when thy heart began to beat,
What dread hand? & what dread feet?

Do dragons breathe fire? *What has made the little fox cough in the meadow of bush clover?*[9] Dragons exist, said Kircher, but they cannot possibly breath fire. Perhaps they are phosphorescent, like some fish, and in the dark of their caves, they do seem to burn.[10]

The poisonous California newt is engaged in an evolutionary war with garter snakes. In trying to counter the garter snake's ever increasing resistance to its tetrodotoxin, it has now become so poisonous that it can kill a human being if eaten by one. It answers threats by bowing up its head and tail to expose its bright orange underside in warning. Eat me and I will stop your breath! St. Augustine:

> *If, therefore, the salamander lives in fire, as naturalists have recorded, and if certain famous mountains of Sicily have been continually on fire from the remotest antiquity until now, and yet remain entire, these are sufficiently convincing examples that everything which burns is not consumed.As the soul too, is a proof that not everything which can suffer pain can also die, why then do they yet demand that we produce real examples to prove that it is not incredible that the bodies of men condemned to everlasting punishment may retain their soul in the fire, may burn without being consumed, and may suffer without perishing?*

In the most famous of Kircher's magic lantern illustrations, the fire of the lamp is projected along with the picture on the slide as a single image, for example: a soul burning in purgatory. He was sure the well-ordered volcanic chambers he had described were created to house those burning souls.[11]

THE TIGER CROP

In the back yard of the house where I grew up, the trumpet vine was always in the process of lifting the tool shed off its foundations and carrying it into the sky. We used to pull off the long flowers to tongue the drop of nectar hidden in their throats.

A bank of hundreds of tiger lilies (ironically enough, highly poisonous to cats). If I placed myself correctly and raised my arms to them as if about to direct a choir, they seemed to look at me with joyful anticipation.

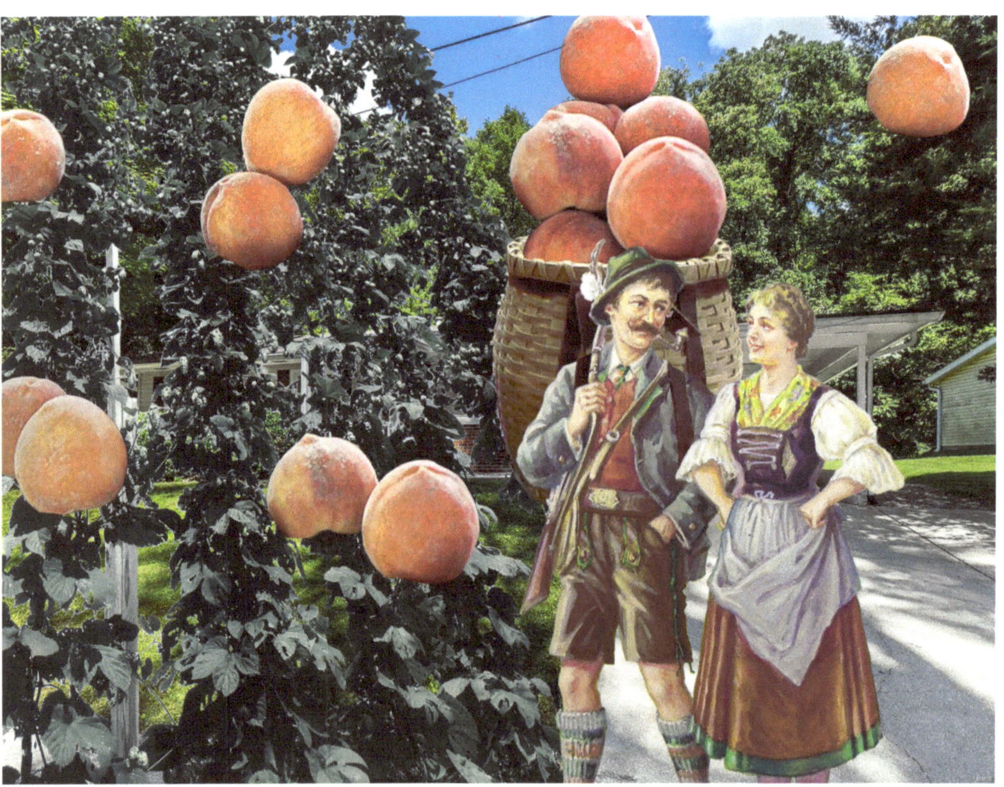

The hop vines in my grandmother's back yard are bearing a bemusing kind of fruit. The vines grow high up and seem attached to nothing; they bear clusters of fruits in various stages of ripening that have the bloom and color of salmon berries. The ripe ones are the size of a fist. And, for no reason, occasionally, a clump of peaches hangs down like a bunch of grapes. Are they from the hop vine as well, or are they the fruit of some kind of mistletoe-like parasite?

The hop vine harvesters are out in force, and they offer to pick fruit for us. I promise them some of the fruit in exchange. They carry crates on their backs piled high with fruit. Once the crates get full enough, the peaches detach themselves and migrates toward them, like to like. Or perhaps the pickers use the shepherd's crooks they carry. In any case, with their lederhosen and their rustic aspect, they are a picturesque addition to the streets of the St. Louis suburbs.

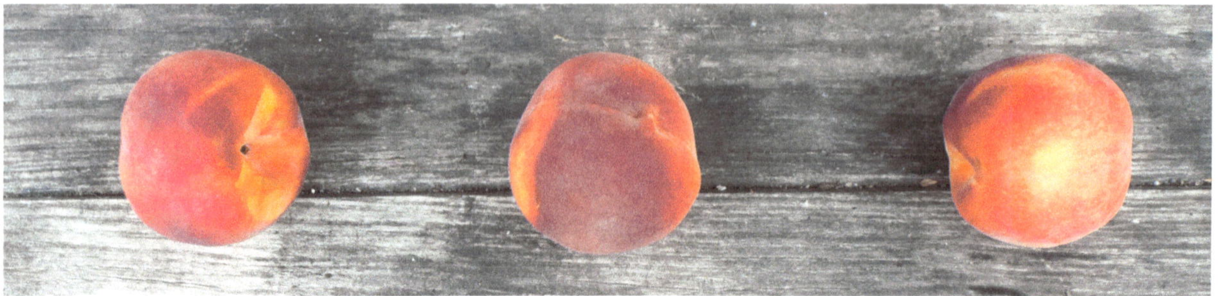

Apricot tangerine cantaloupe mango peach papaya tangelo nectarine jackfruit persimmon loquat kumquat oranges turning into sand turning back into oranges I have picked up off John and Connie's floor and am squeezing for juice because their floor is covered with oranges, but no, it's sand, undulating ridges of it having crept in somehow, from where? The dunes are miles away. No, it's oranges, and a grapefruit. I'm not going to use the grapefruit, and put it back on the floor. Where it turns into sand, and it's moving, and sinking away out of sight, very stealthily. Is the sand simply falling between the floor boards? It seems more sentient than that.

■

A soft lightly unripe rose, an apricot-pink rosé with a white bloom over it. The interior more golden, down to the rose crevasses that cradle the seed. At the grocery store, my mother sniffed at a peach then put it back. No smell no taste, she said.

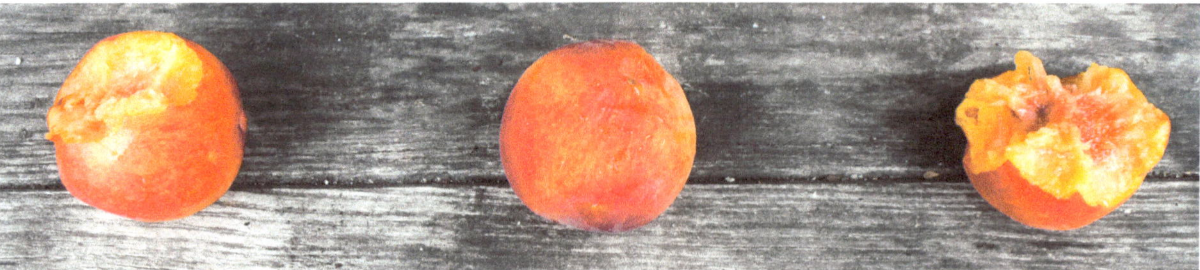

RUBY SULFUR

After his youthful travels, Kircher settled in Rome, the center of the vast Jesuit network to which he had right of access, and collected the incoming streams of information, working all the while to connect this to that. He was, however, traveling past Aetna and Stromboli when their volcanic activity blasted the island of St. Euphemia in 1638, and then through Naples when Vesuvius was starting to show signs of activity. How volatile and alarming the south must have seemed compared to his native Germany. Intrepidly he had himself lowered into Vesuvius's smoking crater; his writing on volcanos at least began from his own observations.[12]

Volcanic Italy is a major source of the arsenic disulfide realgar, the only pure orange pigment before artificial pigments were developed in the 19th century. Found naturally in *kiln-lit funnels, fumaroles, cones, towers,* beloved by alchemists, used medicinally in China *despite its poisonous nature.*

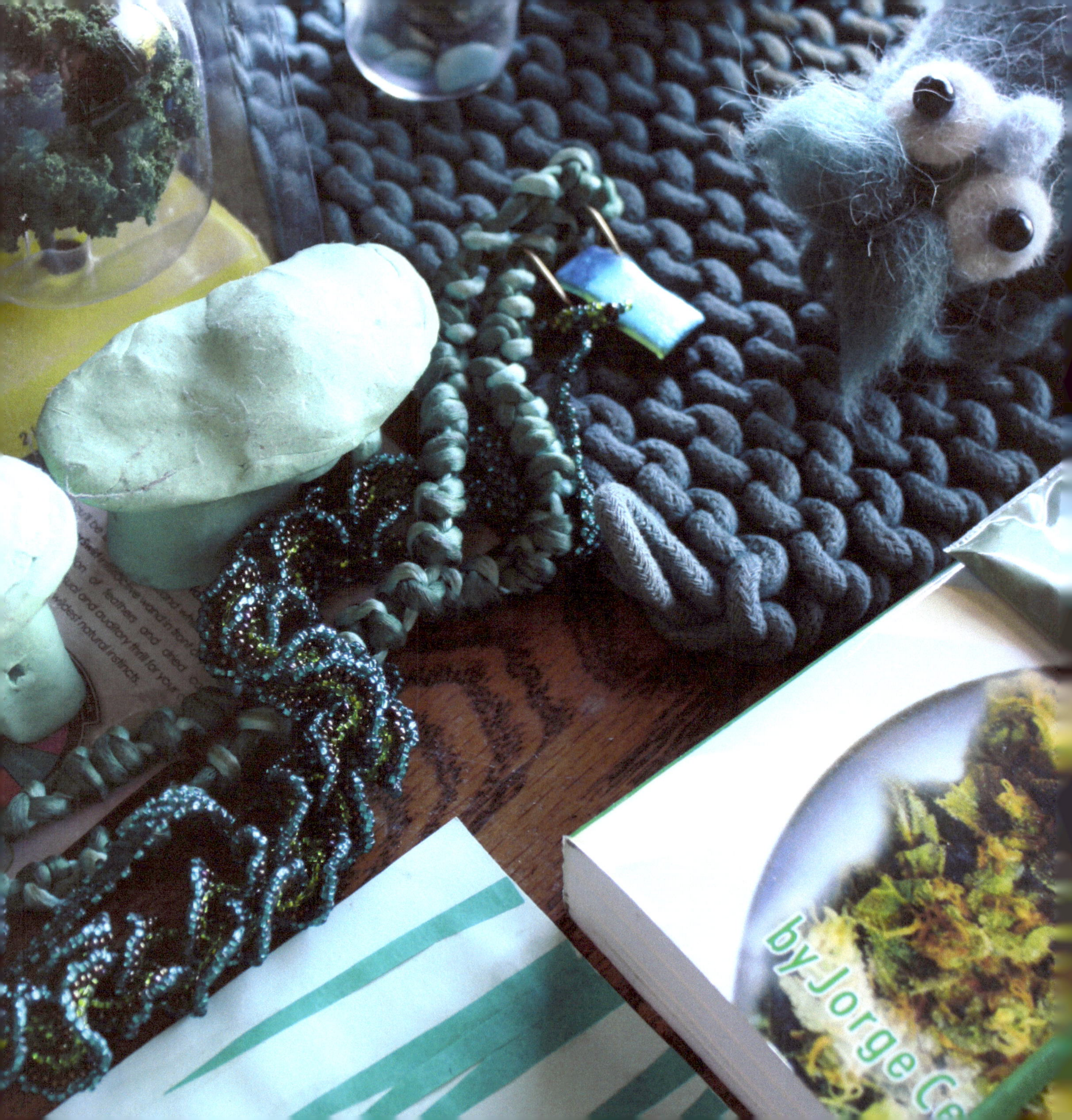
by Jorge Ce

THE CAGED GARDEN

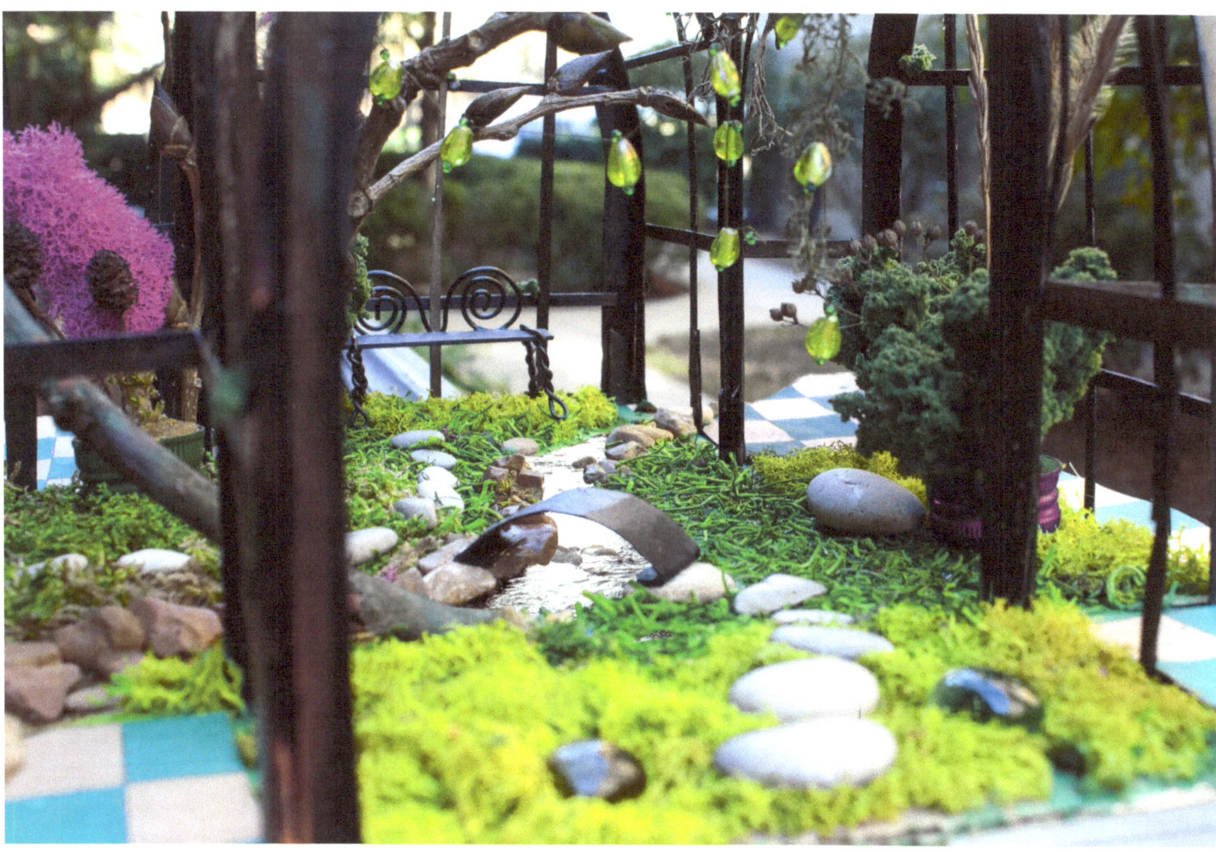

Whenever I visit this wealthy industrial family in their imitation Italian villa, I make sure to visit the small gem-like conservatory set into the courtyard. Usually I have it to myself, but today the young man of the family approaches awkwardly, and awkwardly proposes. I could make a dozen true and tactful refusals—that he's half my age, that I'm married already—but instead I tell him this: that he's too stupid to marry. I think that is kinder somehow. He makes a cutting and quite brilliant reply, ending with: *And* you have an ice cube in your hair. Which I have. Good for him really. Certainly proved me wrong. I do regret passing up a chance at having a conservatory.

PRIMARY SECONDARY

Kircher published this diagram, the work of fellow Jesuit François d'Alguilon, in his *Ars magna lucis et umbrae, The Great Art of Light and Shadow,* in 1646. While Kircher still held to the classical idea that the primary colors were derived from black and white, he showed here that he understood the secondary colors to be combinations of the primary colors. Before this, green had the same status as black, white, yellow, red, and blue; now it was demoted forever.[1]

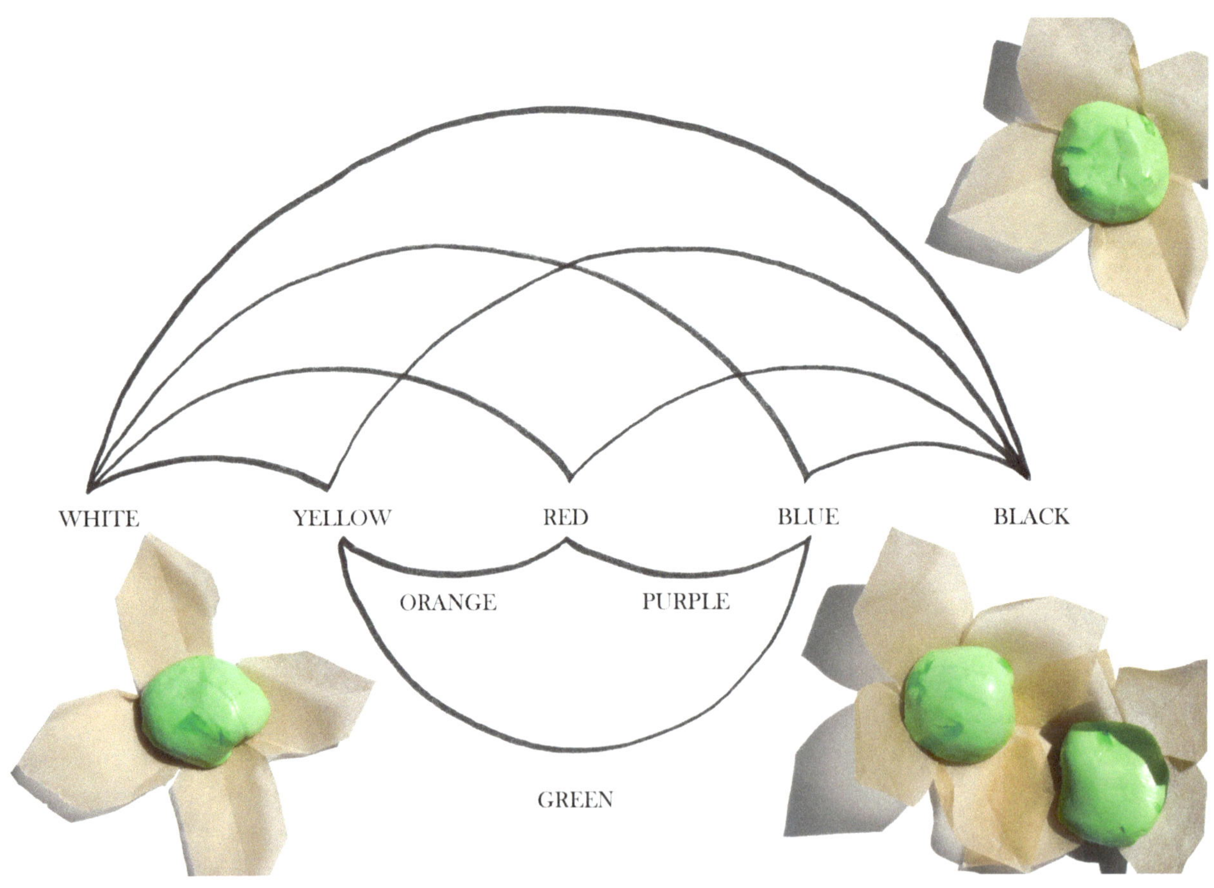

OPERATIC CUCUMBER

I'm attending an opera where each act is performed in a different room of the natural history museum. One act is a restaurant scene, and the performers are seated at a line of tables along a long gallery. The performers are ad-libbing banal conversation and gestures until the music begins. The restaurant food is theatrically rendered on their tables by various arrangements of cucumber peelings—a pile of them for a salad, a few scraps in water for soup. The performers and the audience all keep getting up and milling around and the opera never really begins. Still, there is an intermission. During it, a museum docent invites some of us to look into the observatory. This is against the rules and I am thrilled. In the moat around the observatory, the head of a crocodile is sticking out of the mess of algae. Surely it's a mechanical model? There's no fence, also no room in the moat for the back half of the crocodile.

Here's the door to the observatory, a green rounded triangle sloppily enameled with red and white flowers, as if my dream were already translating itself into a crude diorama. We push open the door and walk in to find, not a telescope, but

■

At the laundromat, we saw a woman with a monk parakeet on her shoulder and a praying mantis of the same green on her head. Occasionally she would pet the bird or take down the mantis and talk to it. Could the flying turtles of Honan really fly? No, said Kircher, but his illustration says otherwise.[2]

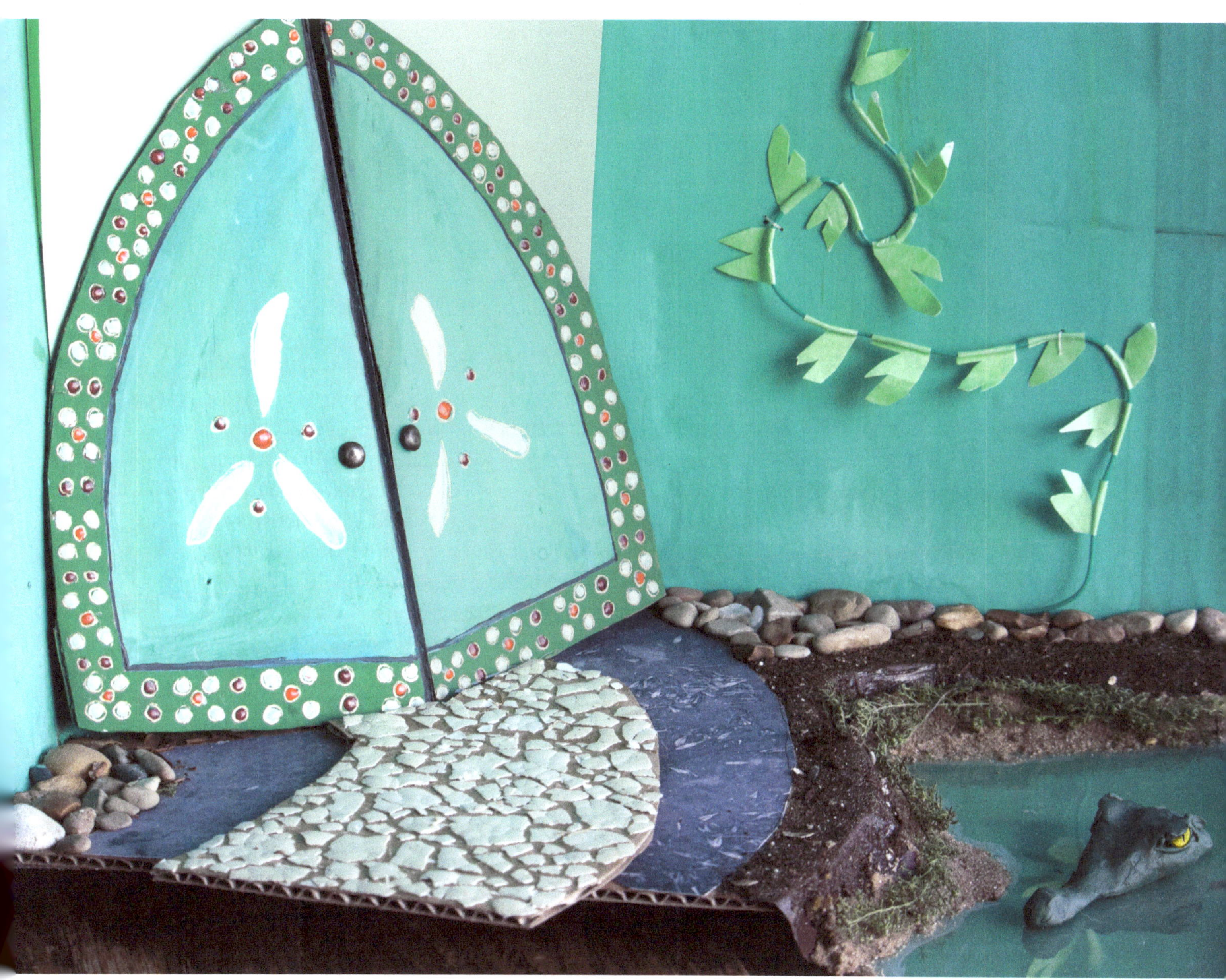

Green shelters and conceals and loops around wrists and ankles. Green proliferates until it chokes on its own abundance.

When lo! I saw a bright green snake
Coiled around its wings and neck.
Green as the herbs on which it couched,
Close by the dove's its head it crouched;
And with the dove it heaves and stirs,
Swelling its neck as she swelled hers!

Writing this book is teaching me what a product I am of colonial history. From eleven to eighteen I lived in a rural town of eight hundred in central Illinois. I read all the time, out of true preference, but also to fill all that spacetime that most teenagers fill with social activities. My desperate idea of a well-read person was mostly derived from poetry anthologies edited by Andrew Lang (gifts from my grandmother). And all my cultural nostalgia and longing for a world in which I would have someone my own age to talk to expressed itself in a very narrow taste for cloying depictions of the Middle Ages, like Howard Pyle's version of Robin Hood, and Midwestern Gothic details on early 20th century churches, and fantasizing about Liberty print wallpaper. I furnished the red cave of my Gothically weird and lonely inner life with the most Edwardian of accoutrements.

I'm not complaining about the friendlessness—I moved away and figured out the rudiments of social interaction eventually (no thanks to Andrew Lang). This book is about color, and being haunted, and I am complaining that I vainly invited in the ghosts of a bunch of English Victorian men (and Howard Pyle). I wanted to be solid and formidable to other people, and I thought they would help. And there's no going back on it now; they are the original layer, the first voices I hear, and I am stuck with this brown company—as horrible as I find their politics, as tedious as I find their religious quibbling, as sure as I am that none of them would give me the time of day if I could go back in time and meet them. I still need to wake up from the 19th century. Even William Morris, for all his leftist leanings,

A terrarium of two small green snakes, and a cage of two rare doves, and I accidentally dump them onto the floor together. A snake attacks one of the birds in midair as they fall. I try to pull it off, and it bites my hand, and as I pull it off of that, another takes its place, then another, and they multiply, so that my hands and arms are festooned with writhing green loops. A cousin comes in with her small child, and a snake immediately bites him on the nose. Those are *poisonous,* I say in a temper, pulling it off. So far no one acts poisoned, and the snakes have survived my handling, but they're all starting to look kneaded and doughy, as if they were made of modeling clay…

> Kircher did not approve of magic, in the sense of supernatural observations. But his Hermetic world view, based on the correspondence of all levels of being, did allow for influences to travel from higher to lower levels—for example, from the planets to plants and the human body. To exploit these correspondences and to harness the occult or hidden forces in matter was *natural* magic, shading imperceptibly into what we call technology. At the summit of the Hermetic chain of being is the mind of God…[3]

Kircher believed so easily, devoutly that the chain of being arrived at the mind of God. Nor can I believe with Blake that the imagination is synonymous with the World Soul. I labor to content myself with metaphor, analogy, and associative thinking to give me a *possible* vision of a connected world. The dragonfly had *turquoise dots all down its back like Lauren Bacall.* The chime of shared characteristic or impression, the more precious for being intuitive and difficult to explain, gives us an aesthetic if not a metaphysical net of connections to keep the world from flooding in and driving us all insane.

THE GRASS HOUR

Monochromatic meals. As I said, some chance combinations of tastes did turn out well, like pistachio cookies with matcha. Other ideas entertained and discarded: the colors associated with planets, chakras, gems, flags, heraldry…

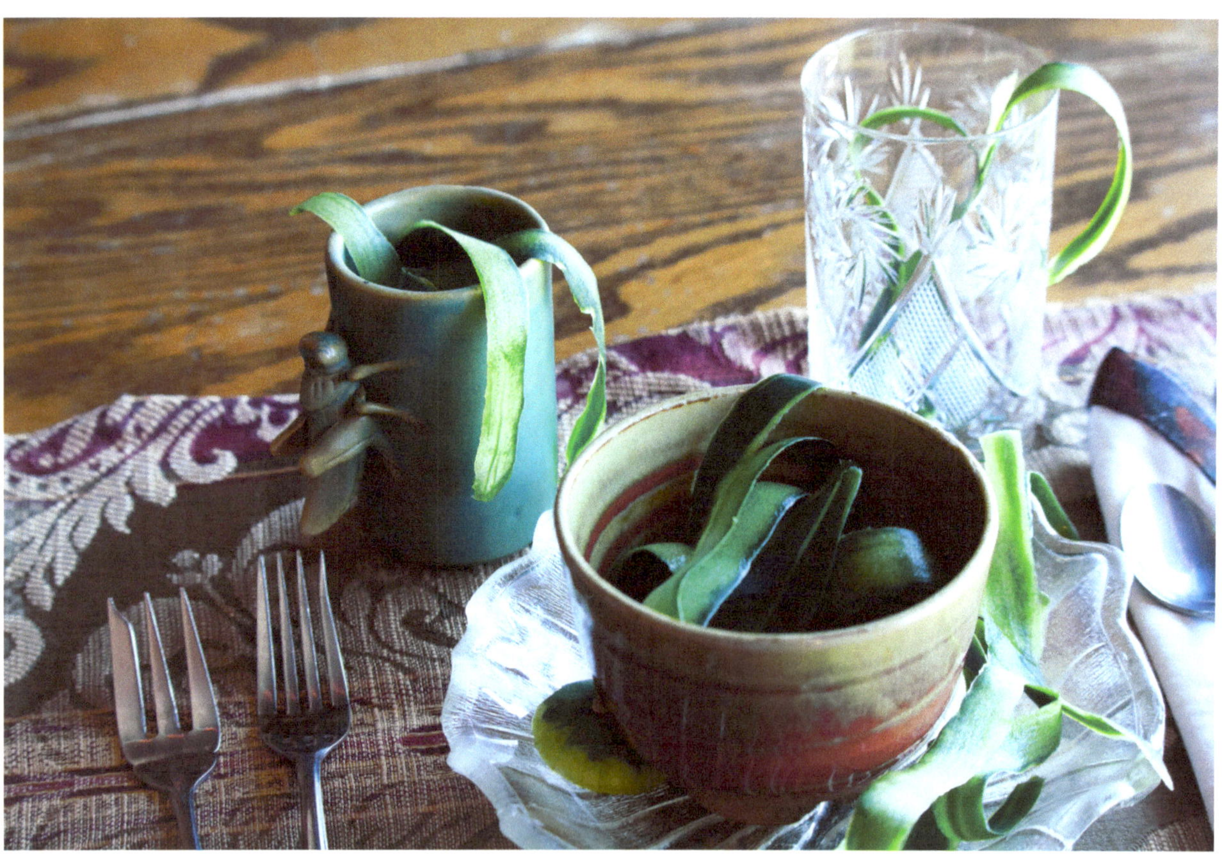

And what are these berries or pods that fill the desk drawers? Tomatillo toffees. They're faceted like gems within their papery leaves. (But when I tried to press facets onto the green apple taffy I was using, the sides wouldn't stay flat. Taffy is a liquid, it turns out, albeit a very viscous one. Also, I couldn't keep from eating my illustration. There again, the sticky indiscriminate imitation fruit glue on my teeth, and I was nine, walking the blocks—so many!—home from the candy store, with my allowance converted into a small paper bag heavy with colors. Only nostalgia could savor that painful concentration of sugar.)

■

The Candoshi of Peru have no word that means 'color.' Instead of asking 'what color is it,' one asks, 'what is it like?' Which will be answered, like blood, like tar, like an unripe fruit.[4] Imagine a language in which color is always embodied.

Self portrait through plants. Here is a page of Werner's greens, for example, as they occur in the planters of my balcony, in the light of a hazy noon day in late June in Chicago:

Celandine Green: Under-leaves of Sweetpea

Mountain Green: Dill Leaves

Leek Green: Spearmint Leaves

Blackish Green: Steams of Thai Basil

Verdigris Green: Leaves of Thai Basil (although a little less blue)

Bluish Green: Lavender Leaves

Apple Green: *Grow the Rushes,* Leaves of Summer Savory

Emerald Green: Sweet Basil

I'm thinking about colors when the day is cloudy. Under that close ceiling, the green fire of the grass banks and deepens. Or when the sun is otherwise obscured. One afternoon, during a partial eclipse, we were beneath a silver maple, each tiny space between leaves its own camera obscura. Hundreds of crescents projected onto the dappled sidewalk, so that it looked like we were standing on water.

Kircher, fascinated by optical illusions of all kinds, included in *Ars Magna Lucis* a drawing of a grassy landscape that revealed itself, in Arcimboldo fashion, to be a face when turned on its side. The forest was a beard, the eyebrow ridge a mountain, the nose a distant tower.[5]

Six years old *when summer first was leafy,* a cloudy evening in June, the beginning of summer vacation. My favorite television show would be on in half an hour. I asked my mother to call me at seven o'clock exactly, and went out to the back yard. My sister and I played on the swings under the cloudy sky as my father cut the grass. When I finally went back in, it was long past seven. My mother had forgotten my request and was puzzled that I even minded, opening up one of those abysses of betrayal and disappointment that are only possible at that age. But let me remember instead what I got: a half hour of anticipation that lasted impossibly on and on with the endless light of the green evening; the safely contained fenced-in box of the back yard; my father an engine sound and the smell of cut grass; the creak of the swings; the ability to be wholly absorbed by nothing in particular.

Leaving the mosquito netting and walking out of Nara: the young leaves…[6] The human eye sees more shades of green than any other color. It's an omnivore's vision, both eyes facing forward as a predator, registering the prey's distance, registering with our concentrations of cones all the intervals between ripe and unripe fruit, but it's also the vision of possible prey. What is that face among the trees.

A SCRAP OF WALLPAPER CRACKS THE GREEN-GLAZED POISON PLATE OF CERAM

Whites, golds—let us now consider Japanese screens and their use of green. Think of their lichens, willow leaves, hills of young grass emerging from mist. The best pigment uses malachite, which "is typically associated with copper deposits around limestones," and has the mineral habit of accreting in crevasses in botryoidal globules. What about that pigment, slightly blue, slightly ashy, feels greener than pure green? It seems to rest on a different plane than the less opaque washes around it. It partakes of the new pine needles or grass that it depicts, but it's also powdery, light and adherent as pollen, a dull matte so soft that seeing it is like being stroked by it.

> So malachite can occur in botryoidal formations, which means 'like bunches of grapes.' Is That Not Cool.
>
> Malachite Mulligan, said Bobby.
>
> Who's that?
>
> Malachi Mulligan, you know, plump stately Buck Mulligan…
>
> Buck Mulligan's real name was Malachi?
>
> Hmm. Real name? I don't know if you understand this, but Buck Mulligan is one of those, what do you call them, fictional characters.
>
> I teach creative writing for a living I know what a fictional character is bite me.

■

owed much of his success to arsenic. Making arsenic-laced green wallpaper gave lung ailments to factory workers, not to mention the miners employed by the arsenic mining company he partly owned. Humidity caused a vapor to rise in green rooms that sickened and killed his customers also. Morris was singularly uninterested in this danger, calling the arsenic scare "witch fever."[7]

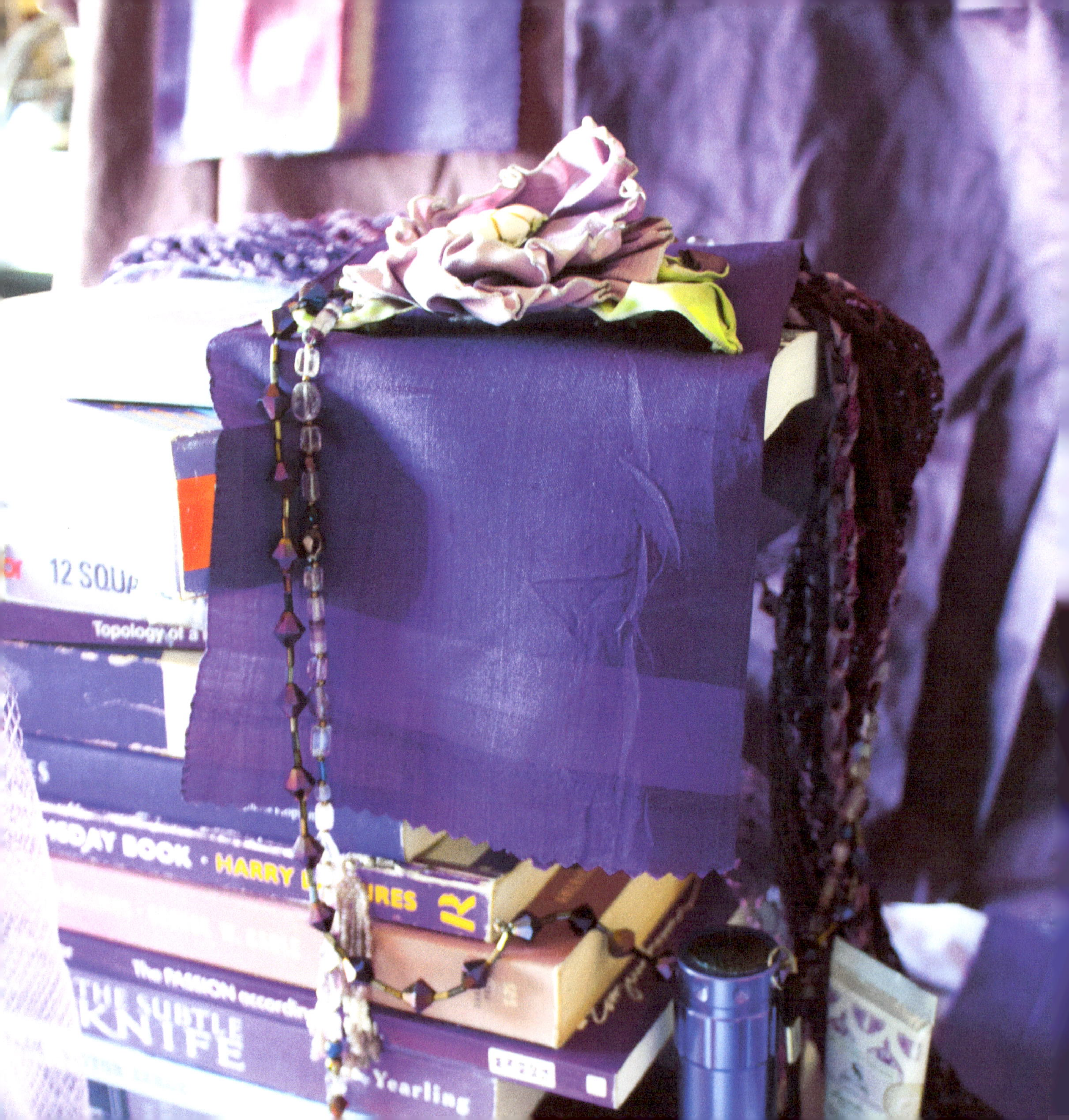
Topology of a
DAY BOOK
HARRY
THE SUBTLE
KNIFE
Yearling

ALIEN LAUNDRY ROOM/ART GALLERY

My mother made dioramas for birthday presents, Christmas. We just called them boxes. They were our fantasies given miraculous materiality. I had a mermaid's bedroom with seaweed curtains of iridescent green beads; later a room in the palace on the moon, where everything was silver and white. Also a village of toadstools, each with a tiny house inside. In play, the most mundane domestic tasks, cooking, sleeping, become magically strange when done in a strange setting, and the boxes staged that transmutation. We played with them until there was nothing left of them.

Once I requested a box set on an alien planet where everything was purple. For once, my imagination and my mother's diverged—the room looked like a typical 70's vision of the future. *Transformed into inhabitants of Saturn.* And the purples she used were wrong, not at all what I was waiting for. But this was The Sole Disappointing Box. I remember the interior of those boxes more vividly than any room I ever lived in.

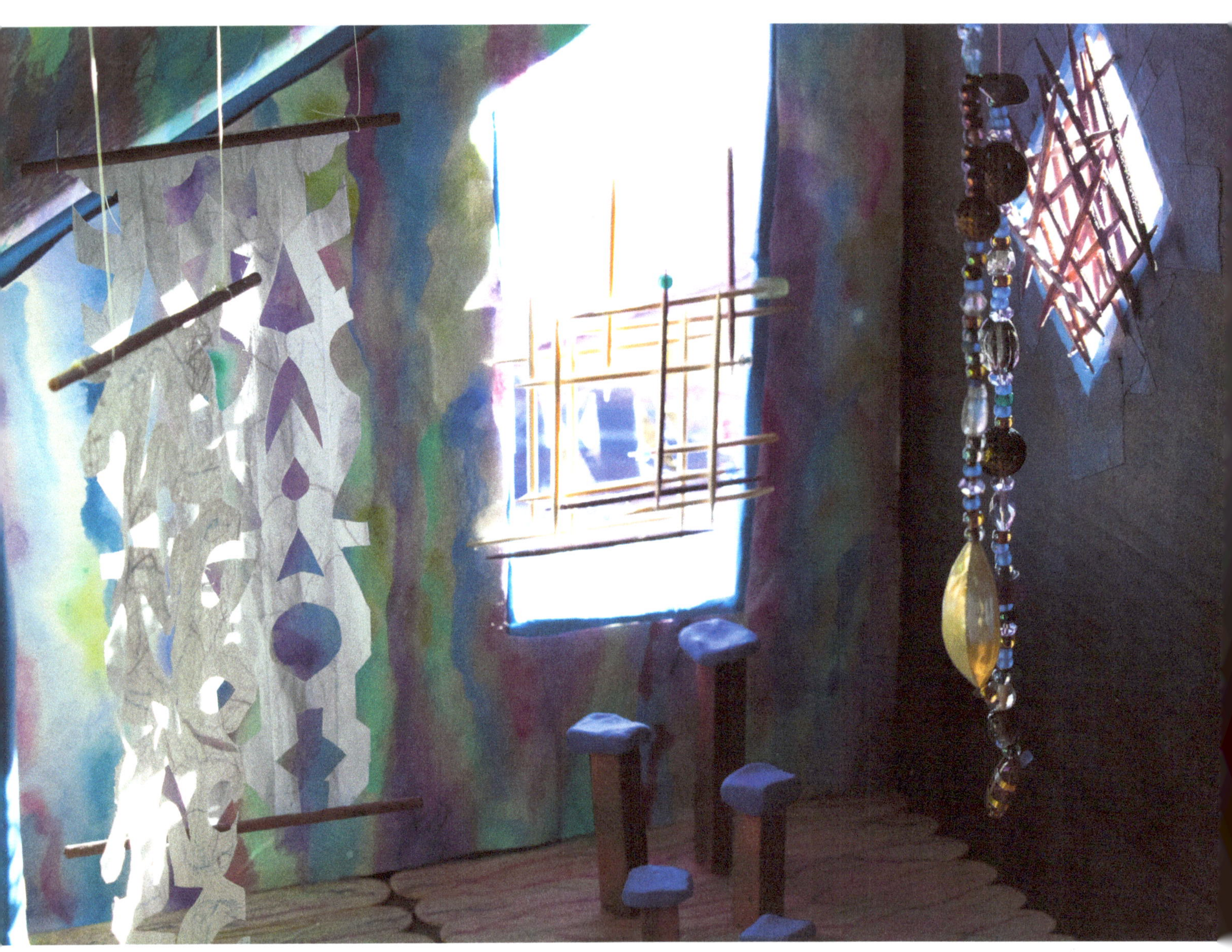

HAN TYRIAN ROYAL PATRIARCH VERONICA ELECTRIC PSYCHEDELIC

Red-purple drowns, like wine. Blue-violet is a dark light on the refracted edges of things. Kircher didn't see purple in the rainbow; the color wheel was only completed with Newton. This is not a judgement on Kircher—cultures divide and name the colors of the rainbow very differently. There's nothing definitive about our six, or Newton's seven. Some medieval paintings give it only two. (I think medieval painters were often trying to convey that the rainbow was luminous, rather than colorful.)

While the west knew and valued red-violet, and strove for millennia to dye cloth in that color, violet tending toward blue was a jarring and newfangled obsession of the Impressionists. By leaning into this liminal color, they taught us to notice it, once we got over the shock. Color of morning twilight, evening twilight, especially in April, when the lengthening day is still surprising: look out expecting night and instead see the lavender sky, the windows just beginning to glow yellow.[1]

The gaps between languages have given valuable gifts, leek blue skies and apple-tawny horses. The Greeks almost certainly did not mean that the ocean was purple like wine. But we carry around a picture of a Greek ship on an intoxicatingly purple Mediterranean Sea.

DasSarma's Purple Earth Hypothesis proposes that the beginning of life may have been purple halobacteria or something like it, harvesting light by means of retinal rather than chlorophyl. Perhaps the sea was once wine dark with it. Chlorophyl would have evolved later to harvest the light that the purple life forms did not use, but once it thrived, it generated enough oxygen to wipe out the purple and replace it with green. In searching for life on other planets, we have been looking for absorption of red and blue light, for green-reflecting chlorophyl, but we should look also for the absorption of green-yellow light, because a retinal-based ecosystem, a purple alien planet, if you will, is also possible.

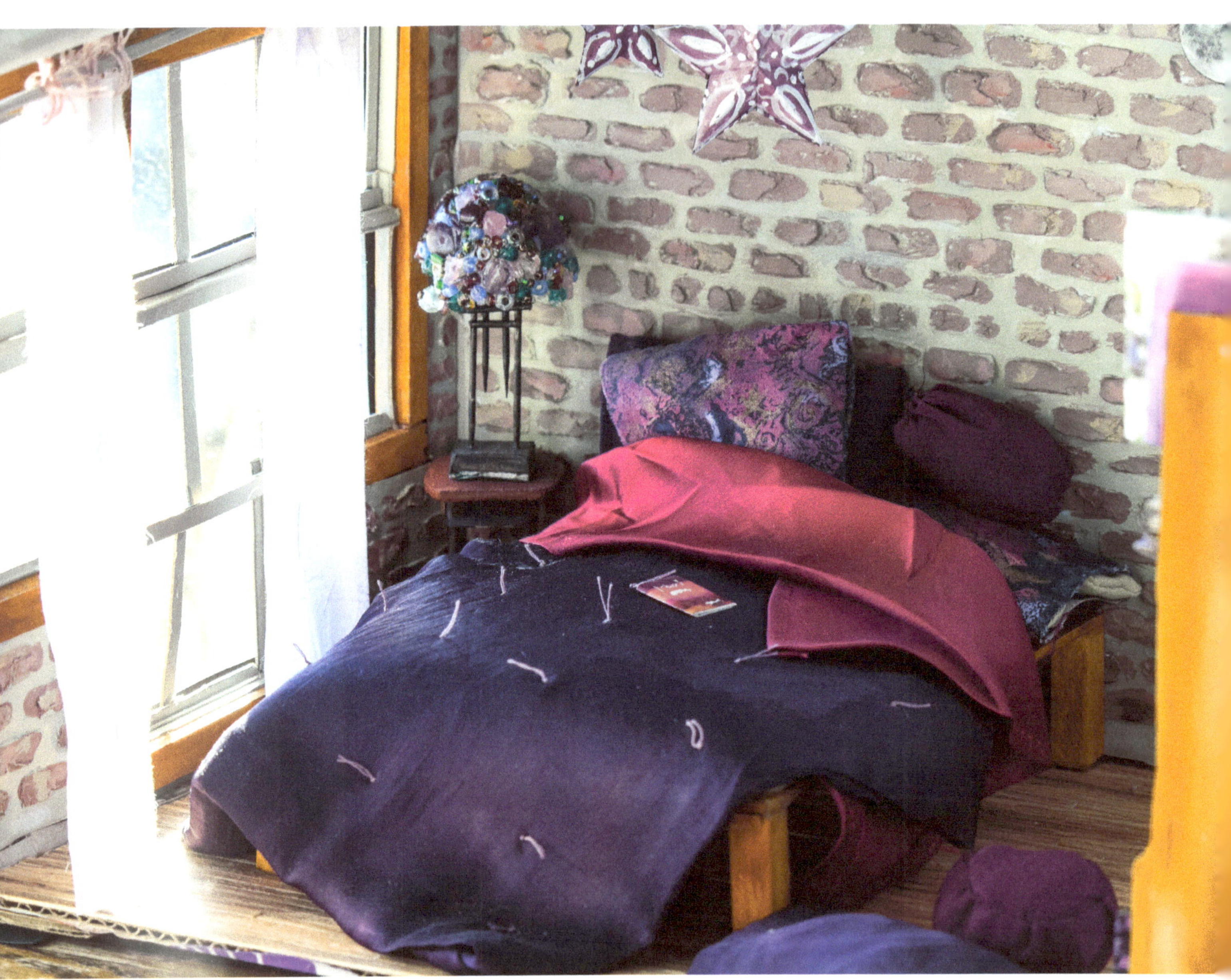

THIS IS HOW I SLEEP

The rest of the time, the room itself sleeps, its objects resting in relation to each other, curtain and sheets, light purple dark purple, patterned and plain, crumpled and smooth…

Dawn twilight: a lavender curtain lifts in the spring breeze.[2]

Empty rooms. Those long takes in Ozu movies, when the wind blows the curtain, and the birds rustle in their cage, and the chair and table and open book sit waiting… it's more suggestive of human habitation, of its moods and unreflective silences, than anything that happens once a character walks through the doorway.

> *There are few of us who have not sometimes wakened before dawn, either after one of those dreamless nights that make us almost enamoured of death, or one of those nights of horror and misshapen joy, when through the chambers of the brain sweep phantoms more terrible than reality itself, and instinct with that vivid life that lurks in all grotesques, and that lends to Gothic art its enduring vitality, this art being, one might fancy, especially the art of those whose minds have been troubled with the malady of reverie. Gradually white fingers creep through the curtains, and they appear to tremble. In black fantastic shapes, dumb shadows crawl into the corners of the room and crouch there. Outside, there is the stirring of birds among the leaves, or the sound of men going forth to their work, or the sigh and sob of the wind coming down from the hills and wandering round the silent house, as though it feared to wake the sleepers and yet must needs call forth sleep from her purple cave. Veil after veil of thin dusky gauze is lifted, and by degrees the forms and colors of things are restored to them, and we watch the dawn remaking the world in its antique pattern. The wan mirrors get back their mimic life. The flameless tapers stand where we had left them, and beside them lies the half-cut book that we had been studying, or the wired flower that we had worn at the ball, or the letter that we had been afraid to read, or that we had read too often. Nothing seems to us changed. Out of the unreal shadows of the night comes back the real life that we had known. We have to resume it where we had left off, and there steals over us a terrible sense of the necessity for the continuance of energy in the same wearisome round of stereotyped habits, or a wild longing, it may be, that our eyelids might open some morning upon a world that had been refashioned anew in the darkness for our pleasure, a world in which things would have fresh shapes and colors, and be changed, or have other secrets…*

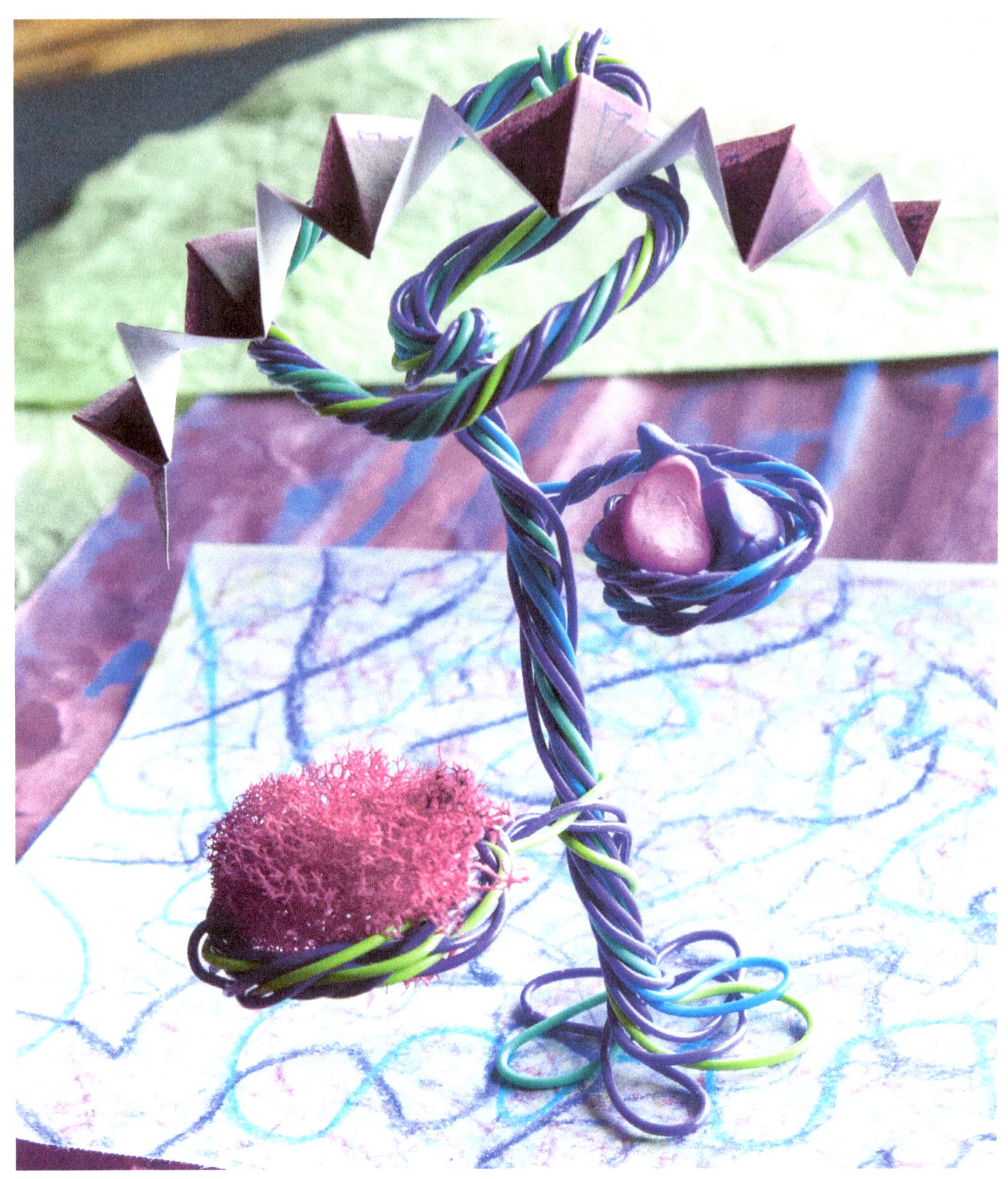

(an alien reading desk)

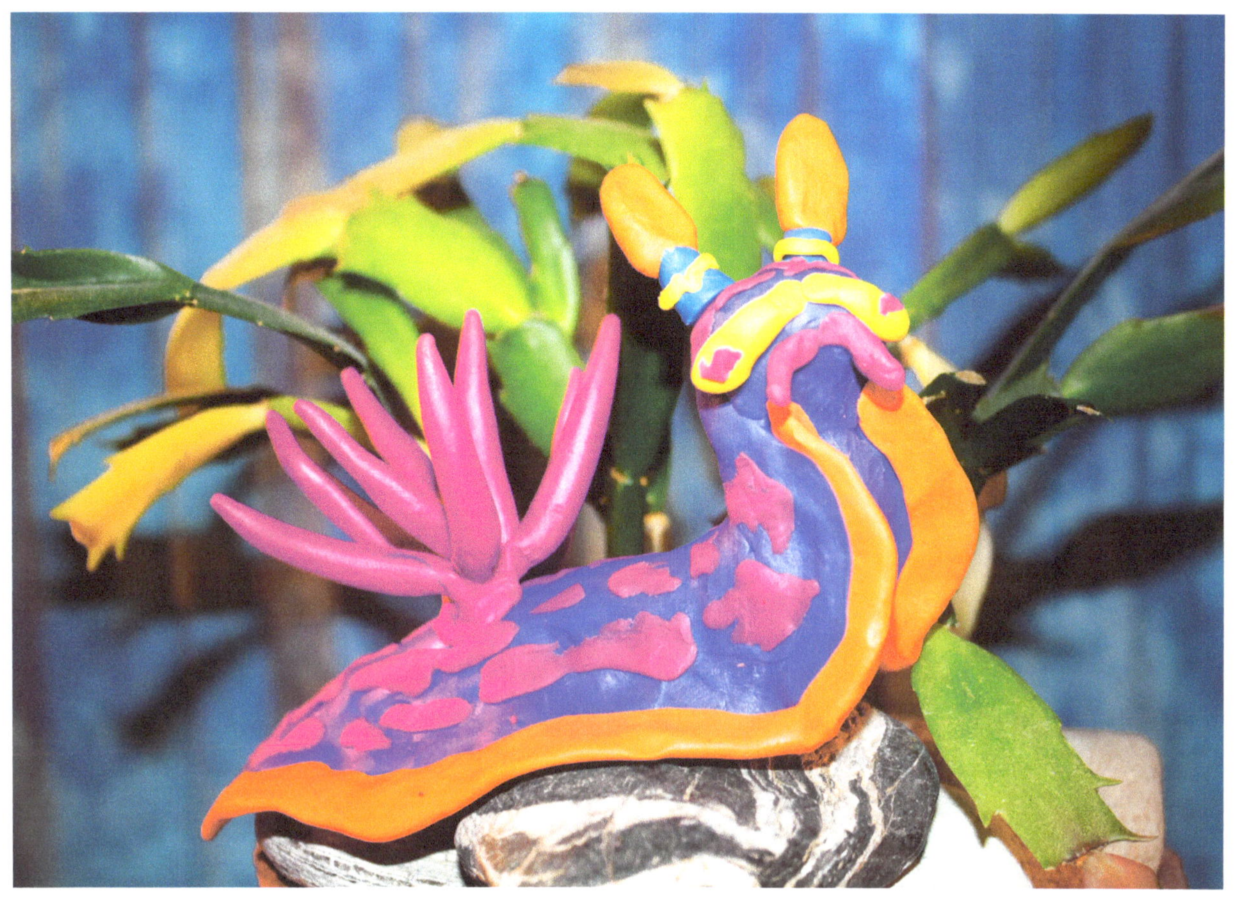

FRANKENSTEIN'S NUDIBRANCH

I have aggregated, but not exaggerated, several species of nudibranch.

Which I collected by commanding my computer to show me the most colorful animals. My computer being a straw sucking energy from the ground. Except in this analogy, the straw also produces poisonous brine sulfuric acid benzine radium and runoff of globe-warming methane (to name a few of the possibilities), all of which enables my search engine to pull a colored thread from the ever diminishing tapestry of the globe's fauna. Siamese fighting fish, peacock cichlid, rainbow blanket octopus, mandarin goby, mantis shrimp—like Jane Eyre in her alcove, I can luxuriate for hours at a time in the parade of images across the screen... Like Kircher and his museum, I am collecting and arranging and celebrating the marvels I am simultaneously helping to erase. Even this looking is a kind of predation.

■

The rods of the human eye give us our night vision due to the presence of rhodopsin, also called visual purple (although it's actually more of a pink—from Greek *rhódon,* 'rose,' and *ópsis,* 'sight'). In our world of plentiful light, rods don't get much of a workout. Spend thirty minutes in near darkness, the level of starlight with no moon, and you'll see that you can see quite well, well enough to read even, but no colors. No rainbow on the octopus.

SO MANY PURPLE FLOWERS ARE TOXIC:

Clematis, delphinium, foxglove, heliotrope, hydrangea, hyacinth, jimson weed, monkshood, wisteria. And many purple flowers can be convinced to give up their water-soluble anthocyanin pigments to dye cloth: iris, hyacinth (again), hollyhocks, hibiscus, lady's bedstraw, purple cinquefoil. In haiku, flowers are a succinct way to dye the poem. That way, a palette is implied without wasting the syllables to name it. *Evening after evening in the soundless rain: a poison iris. When from the beached boat stepping out—edible violets…*[3,4] Taste of sweet earth. Having sliced some boiled beets, I found an abstract masterpiece in magenta left behind on the cutting board.

■

Lucy, who lives with us, confesses that she crashed her car into mine while she was pulling out of a downtown underground parking lot, a completely random coincidence. I left it there months ago, not wanting to drive it home what with not being able to drive. But it was *parked,* I say, incensed. How could you just hit a parked car. Come on now, says Bobby, we've all been there. This is him being tactful, because of the two of us, only I have in fact been there.

I go downtown to inspect the damage, and perhaps get the car home somehow, but first I must visit the restaurant above the parking garage. They serve cake. Mauve rose cupcakes piled high with icing. Also three layer lavender cake with blueberry glaze, also cream chocolates with the papery scent of violets, cakes in every stage of missing slices, fresh to stale and collapsing, great ruins of cake, all in different shades of purple, in a display case that seemingly expands back infinitely as I peer into it.

■

What color do you most want to eat?

Brianna: Purple.

What color is the most poisonous?

Brianna: Purple. Well, that's just disturbing.

Pull off the purple sheet of cardboard that cuts off access to the first ladder up the resonating crystal… Tell me who (or what) you haunt, and I'll tell you who you are. Tell me what you return to obsessively, and I'll use those obsessions to give you back your portrait. But at least in English, the phrase allows for a valuable ambiguity. To whom (or what) do you appear as a ghost? Who is haunted *by* you? I am sure that my climbing up the ladder to look is one of the things the resonating crystal is translating into fractals…

Near the Great Divide, far up in the mountains, I found a fringed gentian. It was small and kept its color deep, almost into black. I thought of Lawrence's gentians, Persephone's lamps lighting the way to the underworld like the lines of blue violet lights along taxiways in night airports. But I tried not to think of them too much, because no one wants their immediate experiences to get completely sucked into some cultural historical vortex, especially not the Charybdis that is D.H. Lawrence. The flower was still closed, the fringed edges of the petals like lashes of a closed eye.

Bees also have trichromatic vision, but unlike us their cone sensitivities are spaced evenly and extend into the ultraviolet. Their flowers are marked with extra alluring spots, runway lights (pick me, land here); their colors round the corner and wander off to where we cannot see them.

TRUE KNOWLEDGE OF THE DRUNKEN AMETHYST

Making coal gas produced the byproduct of coal tar, so there was a lot of it lying around. Quinine, on the other hand, was scarce, and the work of empire was causing a lot of Englishmen in tropical climates to die of malaria. In 1856, William Perkin, while trying to find a way to make quinine from coal tar, poured alcohol into a test tube to clean out a gummy black failure, and was startled at the brilliant lilac accident that resulted. Within a few years, he had dyed London mauve. The first aniline dye, mauvine, was so instantly and completely popular that it became a cliché just as quickly *Never trust a woman of any age who wears mauve,* said Oscar Wilde. *It always means they have a history.* Cough cough. We know now that aniline is a 'probable human carcinogen' and 'very toxic.' According to the Environmental Protection Agency, aniline's short- and long-term effects mostly affect the respiratory system…[6] Purple can stop the breath, annoy the lungs, deaden the blood.

■

Kircher recorded as true knowledge that amethysts help to cure drunkenness, and that a snake in India bears a stone in its head that can cure poisonous snakebite. Like connects to like, cure by association. But we have this: dizzying knot ("this dizzying know," I first mistyped) of associative connections and analogies, some clichéd and obvious, others completely eccentric. We all share in the *savage, changeful, natural, grotesque, rigid, redundant* making of revolutionary ornament for some larger building we cannot see. Here is mine:

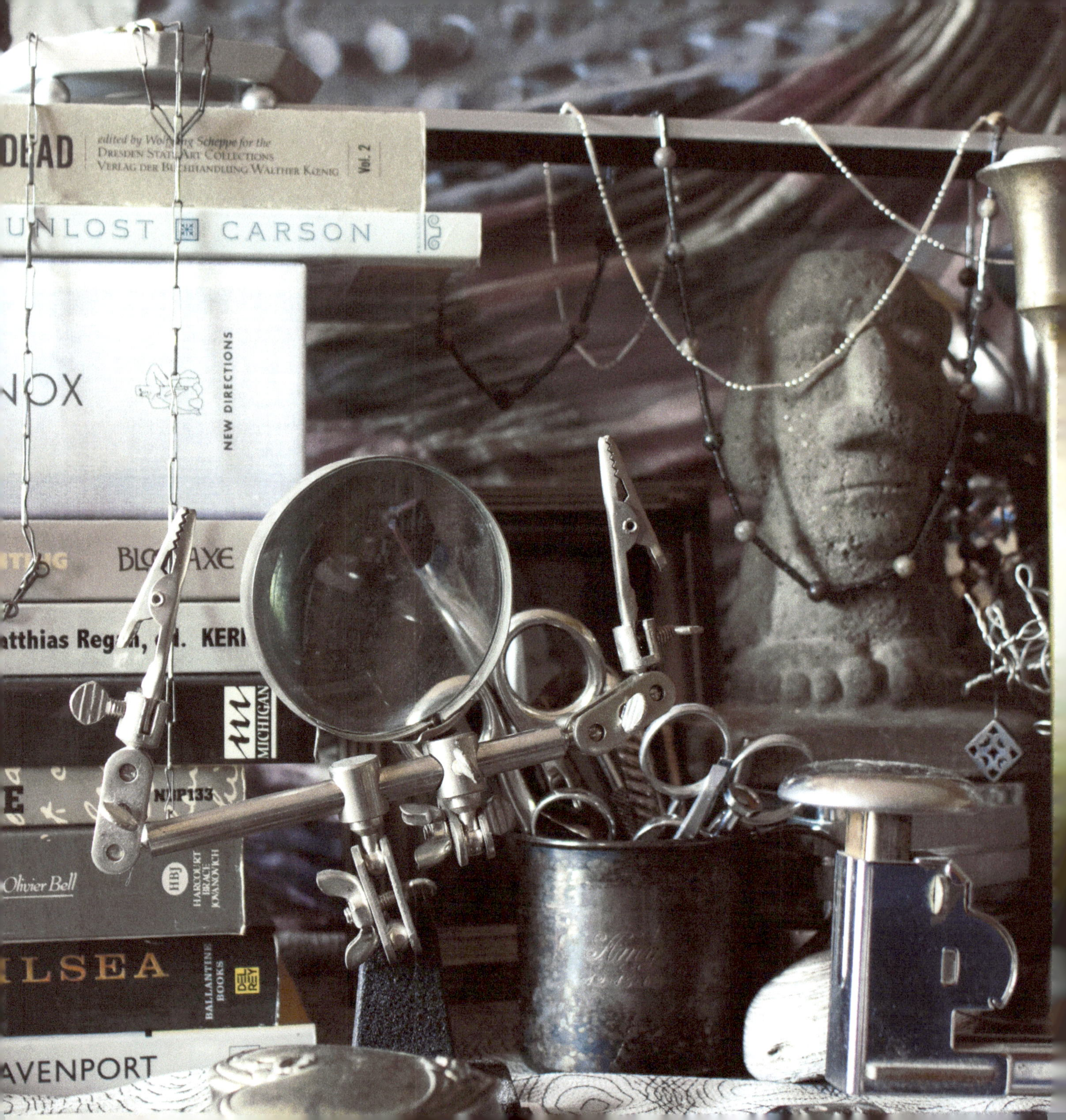

DEAD
edited by Wolfgang Scheppe for the
Dresden State Art Collections
Verlag der Buchhandlung Walther König
Vol. 2
UNLOST
CARSON
NOX
NEW DIRECTIONS
MICHIGAN
NDP133
Olivier Bell
HBJ
HARCOURT BRACE JOVANOVICH
ILSEA
BALLANTINE BOOKS
DEL REY
AVENPORT

INTERROGATING CHILDREN

Recently, I arrived at this unsatisfactory resolve: if I am not able to picture the future, perhaps I can at least speed up the obsolescence of the present. Perhaps I can depict my class and its passivity and levels of consumption as the leftover monstrous zombie ghosts of a past order, rather than something to be preserved and projected into the future at all costs.

I was reading Margaret Cohen on Walter Benjamin's effort to refine Marx's relationship between the base of economic structures and the superstructure of culture.[1] Not the camera obscura, as Marx sometimes described it, the base projecting itself clearly (but upside down) as the superstructure. Rather, the superstructure is the phantasm of the base. Which means what? The superstructure is the dream of the base? The ghost? In Los Angeles, we went to the museum of Jurassic Technology's exhibit on Kircher, where a series of lenses projected mirages of people into dioramas of temples, caves, giant lotuses. Given the setting and our ignorance, we did not know if Kircher was a real person or not. Later that evening, I asked my hosts about these terms, dream, phantasm, and the suggestion in Benjamin that the superstructure could go back and influence the base—doesn't that rob the terms base and superstructure of their revolutionary power? One of our hosts said that it would at least be worthwhile to revisit the question. Having agreed that the relationship is circular, cultural criticism now has given itself permission to restrict its examinations to culture, without looking at economics, and this does indeed seem problematic.

Back home, I had this dream: I look in a mirror, and I see a small Arab boy sitting at a table in a shabby room. I know the boy is nowhere nearby, and a complicated series of reflections between several mirrors and windows is giving me this view, but it really appears as though I were looking through a window, or a one-way mirror into an interrogation room. A friend steps up behind me and I say, don't forget you're coming to lunch. The boy says, okay. I laugh, the friend asks why, and I say: It's so strange that the boy can hear me and thought I was talking to him when he is so far away. Then I worry that I have been rude to the boy, and lean earnestly into the mirror saying, but you, you must come to lunch too…

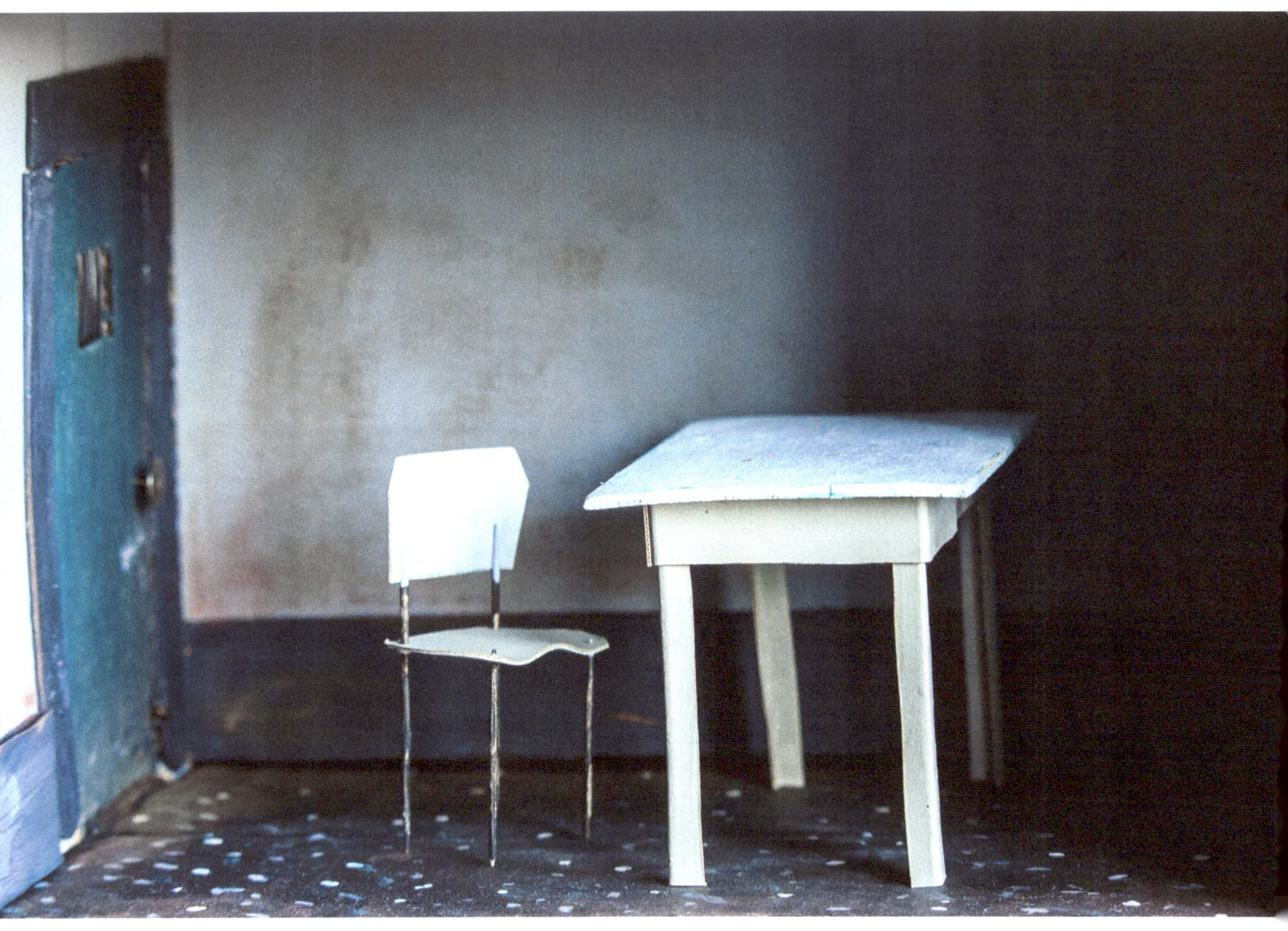

It is lunchtime. The boy's uncle, or maybe it is the boy grown up, has brought a gift—a huge Rube Goldberg contraption of sticks and wheels that he sets up on the dining table. Its cheerful colors and ridiculous embellishments cover the table, but look over the edge, down to the shag carpet. Where Jim is standing, around his feet, the carpet is covered with small crabs, all waving their little claws in the air. Oh no, I say, we have *base*.

When I woke up momentarily, I latched onto this sentence and said it to myself, oh no, we have base, we have base. In the dream, it made perfect sense—*base* being something like lice or mice. Fully awake, I realized that the only recent significance the term had for me was that discussion of Marxist theory. Oh no! The carpet is crawling with economic substructure. It is alien and terrifying and I am chilled to the depths of my petit-bourgeois soul.

And it is as if my dream had shown me the basement rooms where power is enacted (this was at a time when reports of children in Abu Ghurab were starting to filter out), and I had slowly corrected this vision into what I wished were true—the boy is a middle aged man; we are social and economic equals; he is not being interrogated and my duty to him can be fulfilled merely by inviting him to lunch. But the horror is not erased, only displaced into a mysterious unease. The base is still there, under the table, and what do we not deserve from its flood of many claws?

Rereading Cohen, I see that I was mistaken about my ghost. Not phantom or phantasm, but phantasmagoria: a magic lantern, a *mechanism* that projects images, like the camera obscura, but in a way that distorts the image and deludes viewers into thinking they are seeing something supernatural. I have committed the very mistake the phantasmagoria engenders.

Kircher, a real person after all, claimed to invent the magic lantern (thus the projections in the exhibit). And I projected the ghost into Benjamin's writings because it fit with my desires so neatly. How does the base project the superstructure? Before he settled on the analogy of the phantasmagoria, Benjamin used the analogy of dreams. But I think dreams literally do the work of that transmutation. Do that work and warn us of it, encode our suppressed longings and our terrors both into the symbolic order.

According to Pastoureau, the Middle Ages was a long argument about the nature of color—was it made of holy light or fallen matter? But of course our two-chambered minds know it's always both. We talk about pigment versus structural color, but up close enough, all color is structural: all material has structures that reflect back some wavelengths and absorb others. The light of selected wavelengths bounces off objects, through our irises and onto our eye cones: Oh, a red umbrella. But there is no red thing. Of course color is also neither matter nor light. Red is only a certain way of translating data. Only in the brains of certain animals, the outside-in magic lantern brain, does color exist.

I called the friends in LA and told one of them about my dream. They had just become infested with bedbugs which he thought we had brought with us when we visited, and he didn't think the dream was funny, or enlightening, or anything but a horror. Ghostly bedbugs, since the next time we talked (one of the last times we talked) they had remained invisible, and their mysterious bites never reappeared.

YEATS'S GREY

Regarding "The Wanderings of Oisin":

> The colors here are obviously drawn from the Pre-Raphaelite palette with vivid 'crimson' and 'citron' contrasting in their exotic intensity with the pastel and white of the other effects. This becomes the basis of the poem's iterated coloration: 'purple,' 'red,' 'blue,' 'green,' 'silver,' 'gold,' 'golden,' the repeated 'crimson,' along with 'saffron' (orange yellow, etymologically deriving from the French and Arabic) contrast with mixed tints, while the ubiquitous 'white' and the idea of 'whiteness' suggest the Pre-Raphaelite technique of laying down a white base on the canvas so that the enamelled brightness of its colored pigments will be the more intense…after about 1900 Yeats's poetry underwent a striking stylistic revision to make it more syntactically energetic, less rhythmically liturgical and more dramatic. Some of this purging of his poetic involved the eschewal of the kind of color effects that so distinguished his early work. Yeats himself thought this process had begun following the completion of 'The Wanderings of Oisin.' He recalled how 'dissatisfied with its yellow and its dull green, with all that overcharged color inherited from the romantic movement,' he reshaped his style, 'deliberately sought out an impression as of cold light and tumbling clouds' (Au 74)…Padraic Colum recalled being told by Yeats how he was 'trying to get out of his poems the reds and yellows that Shelley had brought back from Italy. Henceforth he was going to try to put into his poems the grays of the west of Ireland, the stones and clouds that belonged to Galway.'[2]

And his poetry fills with greys: *the wave of moonlight glossing the dim gray sands, dew ever shining and twilight grey, the grey round of the hill, the mouse-grey waters flowing, the grey reeds that night and morn are trodden and broken by the herds, the grey rush under the wind and the grey bird with crooked bill…*Sit on the concrete steps as the chill diffuses from toes to feet, works into the haunches, the sharp ends of your bones, and hunch at the wind. Grey is a refusal to see. *Winter rain at Furue—the water's edge disappears…*[3] Grey is invisible toil and its ruinous collapse.

(These are the colors of light I have seen according to place: the blue-white light of Illinois, which is the neutral setting that all others are compared to; the rich gold of the California coast, sister to the yellow light of Turin; the blinding sun of Colorado that strikes the top of your head as if flashed off of a mirror; the pearly air of the Kanto region, like being inside a moonstone; the silver light of Paris illuminating the stone buildings and slate roofs; the orange light of Bangkok casting purple shadows. The light of Ireland is indeed grey, constantly shifting in intensity—now striped with distant rain, now the color of the rain—but not in hue, which tends a little toward blue. It is a grey that sets off, rather than deadens, other colors: the green fire in the grass intensifies; a moment of sunlight makes a sea gull blinding white against the clouds.)

When Yeats was asked, fairies, Oisin, magic: Do you truly believe in these things? He said, They have brought me metaphors for poetry.[4] What does belief even mean then? But while I do not need God or theology to make a connected world, I do require an intact world. All writing seems like elegy now. Goodbye, rooms of my middle class childhood, with their clutter of vacation souvenirs and miniature Oedipus trilogies. Goodbye middle class. Perhaps after our downfall we'll make better alliances.

I can't summon even this glibness to take leave of the natural sources for our images: so many animals, plants, the recognizable succession of weather, seasons…

VISITING MY UNCLE THE MOVIE DIRECTOR, WHOSE HOUSE IS A THEATER

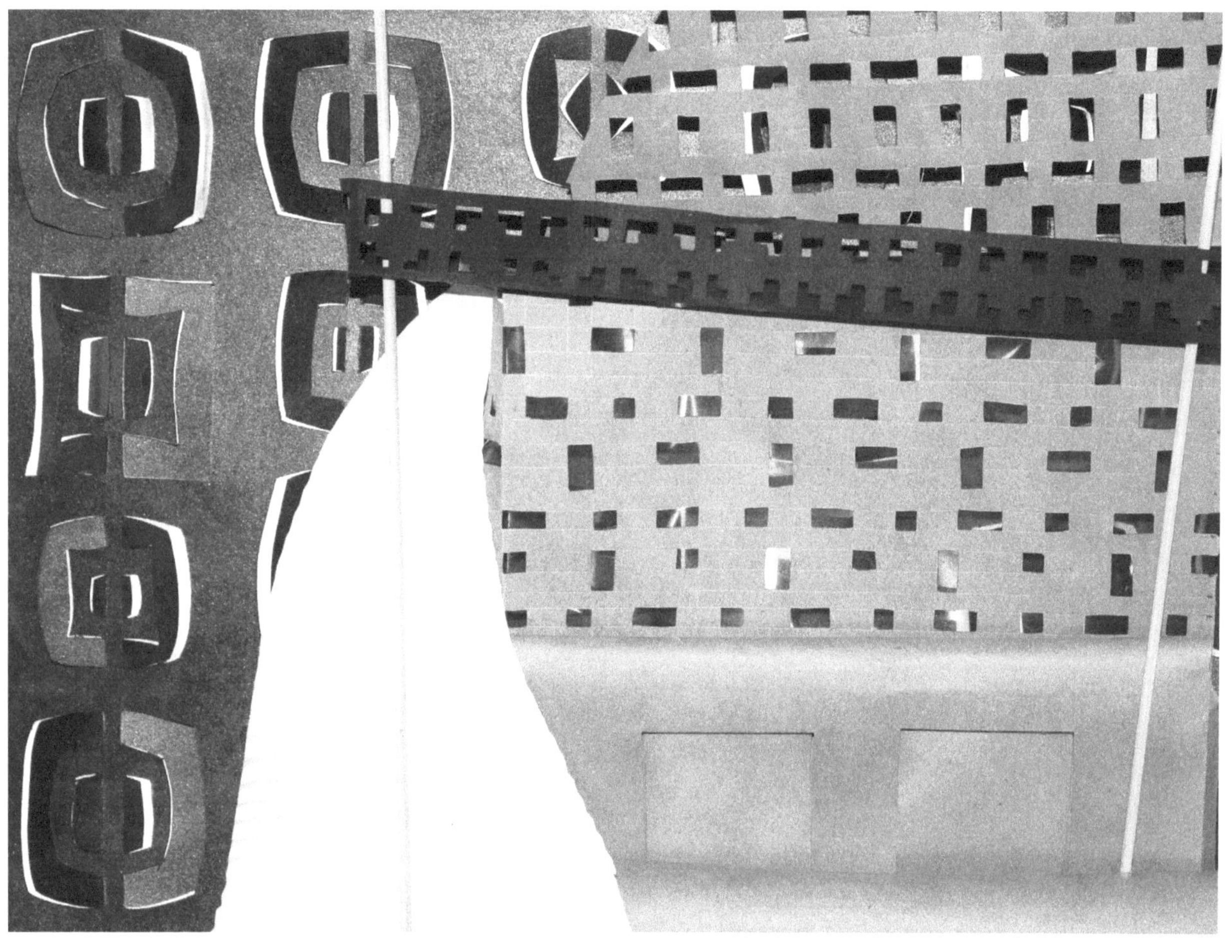

My uncle projects light onto the wall, an old silent film. The workers swarm down the factory steps, then trickle to a few. Now the steps are empty.

NOT A UNICORN

Those horns are not from unicorns, said Kircher, but from some kind of fish.[5]

The professor has assigned us to build an atomic clock. Quite a challenge! especially given my scant knowledge of atomic physics. But now I walk past the Chinese general (in full T'ang dynasty armor) conducting exercises with his magic grey horses. The horses are turning and turning in place, perfect circles with perfectly measured small steps, as precise as cogs on a gear wheel, and I get a brilliant idea. The magic horses can of course be shrunk down to atomic size, and thus they could function as the clockwork of my atomic clock. I would have to shrink with them, and I might not survive it, but if it worked, everyone would be amazed. In my excitement, I start explaining this idea to whoever will listen, imitating in the hallway the small side steps of the horses.

The blue footed booby is refusing to mate in the Galapagos, perhaps due to the loss of sardines, its chief dietary staple.

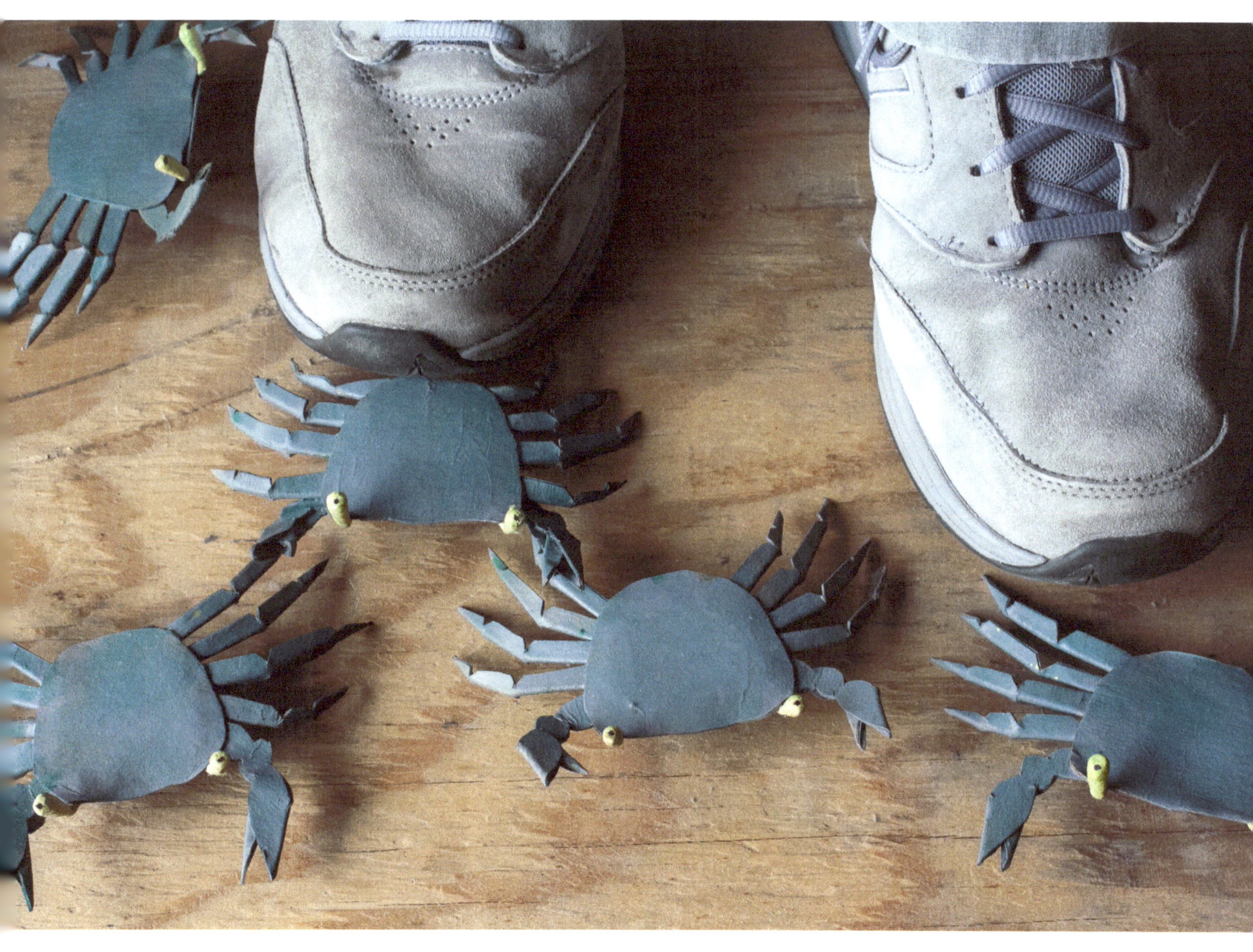

THERE'S GOOD FUNGUS AND BAD FUNGUS

An old wedding cake, dusty, moldy, covered with cobwebs and eaten at by mice, is at the center of the premier phantasmagoria interior of all of Victorian literature, Miss Havisham's Satis House: "the domestic interior itself becomes a 'shining transparency' through which we see into the life of things."[6]

■

When people offer a range of intoxicants, they say, name your poison, and I name you. People who know call you the human hallucinogenic mushroom, and the number of people who know is exactly one, because this is highly specific local knowledge. The intoxicant is you, *tu, du,* and the shaman is me, and that's it, a culture of the smallest possible size.

CIRCULAR METALS

Shelley's paper boat floating in a bowl of mercury. Polishing a sugar bowl and the smell of tarnish. *The short night ending: beside the pillow the folding screen is silver...*[7] A silver-grey scene: looking west down the Chicago River from the lake, and there's the flying Ferris wheel car ferry, the cars on their platforms like Ferris wheel seats staying level as the wheel slowly spins through the air. It occurs to me to wonder where the ferry takes off from. It floats so slowly, and stays so low, threading through the tall buildings—seems like a more local service, like the water taxi. Now the ferry turns right beside Marina City (a very tight, controlled, hovering turn, in midair, more than 90 degrees), and then descends into a docking port on the river that locks onto its points as they circle down. Marina City must give the ferry so much business that it warrants its own docking port. Very local, then. Perhaps other cities don't even have Ferris wheel car ferries.

My shoulder is made of a metal ball joint; the ball is inset with crystal. Inside the crystal is a clock with Roman numerals, some of which are quite sharp. I am relieved to have such a benign explanation for the pain in my shoulder.

An ornately carved limestone mansion, and across the street, a dry limestone fountain. We stand in the corners of the fountain, which are secret elevator platforms that take us underground. (I found the perfect analogue to this mansion online. I was gratified to see that it had been used in a James Bond movie—the tone of the dream is quite Bond-like.)

There, under the mansion, the secret workshop is crowded with tools and the two lab assistants in their lab coats demonstrate the masks they are making. One wears a red *tengu* mask cut out of paper, the other a plastic mask that is just like her own face but slightly too large and slightly the wrong color. They pose themselves on treadmills that move them alternately toward me and away: Paper or plastic? Paper or plastic?

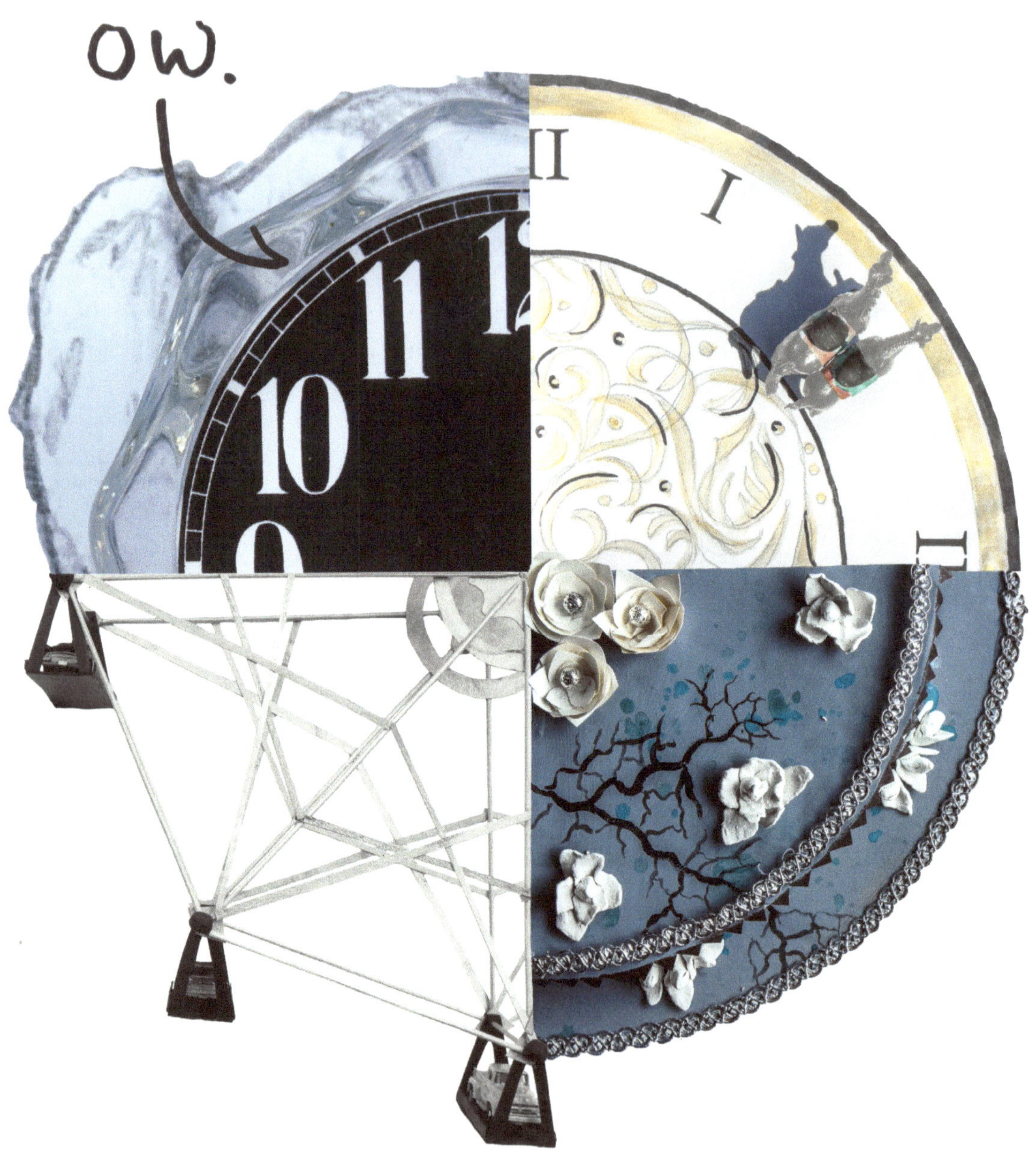
OW.
11
10

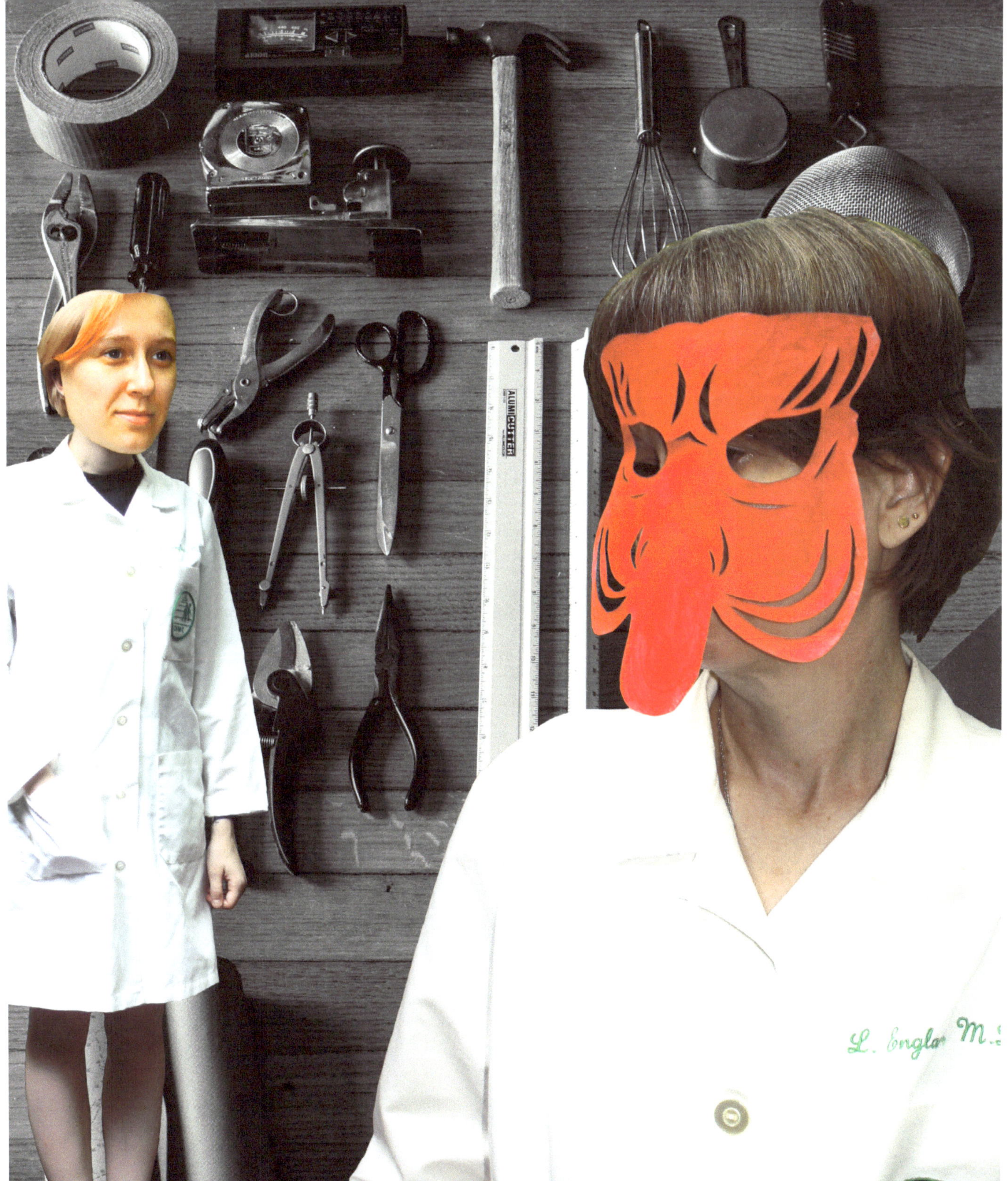
ALUMICUTTER
L. Engla M.

AFTERWORD

The surprise, the way they flash out of black, white, brown, grey. The lavender-green shine on the pigeon's neck. The gaily colored tinker toys out of the herd of grey crabs. Within a few short years, slight alterations to Perkin's formula and process produced from coal tar, in a series of fireworks of fabric visible in draper's shops and dress makers' workrooms and balls, a whole range of dye colors: magenta, bleu de Lyon, Perkin's green…[1] William Morris accused the new dyes of "destroying all beauty in the art," so vulgar compared to the civilized subtlety of good old-fashioned arsenic green.[2] While color was always garish and vulgar, it had become cheap, and therefore thoroughly debased. Now that plastics have increased its range, it is more depraved still.

Western painting history is a long war between color and line. The case against color goes like this: Line is the essential, the true art; color is merely decoration. "In 1810, Goethe…claimed that it is only '*men in a state of nature, uncivilized nations, children,*' who '*have a great fondness for colors in their utmost brightness.*'" Color is childish and other and feminine and frivolous; at the same time, it is a terrible threat, a powerful seduction only to be withstood by the manliest fortitude. Too much attention to it and one's sense of balance and composition will be fatally weakened.[3]

So, having positioned ourselves with the garish, the childish and the debased, having dyed and assembled our skeins of color, let us begin:

In Figure III the two
instruments are combined: as in oleographs, paintings, magic
lanterns, polyhedral glass insets, color is single,
not as a lifeless thing and a rigid
individuality, but a frame filled
with triangular prisms to turn the sunlight entering
a dark chamber into a winged creature that flits
from one form to the next… "You will never have seen

anything like it" children like

the way colors shimmer in subtle shifting supernatural nuances
or else substitute for the opaqueness of my walls
an impalpable iridescence so beautiful that Kircher
likens it to soap bubbles...AB is
a revolving frame with a revolving spectacle
of stars colored like emeralds, sapphires, amethysts,
gold: breaks in the manner of the master-builders
and glass-painters of gothic days the light in-

to a vision of Paradise [4]

And I was walking home, again with my red umbrella, and there was that SMELL of ozone and wet earthy minerals, when I looked behind me and saw the full arch of a rainbow, distinct from end to end. I'd never seen a rainbow and hadn't quite believed in them before. "[Color's] spectrum of effects—uncertainty, confusion, disorientation, delirium, pleasure, delight, wonder—only becomes possible, it seems to me, if color's connection to the world is in the first place provisional and uncertain."[5] As I kept turning to walk away and the rainbow did not recede, I became convinced it was chasing me and ran home in terror.

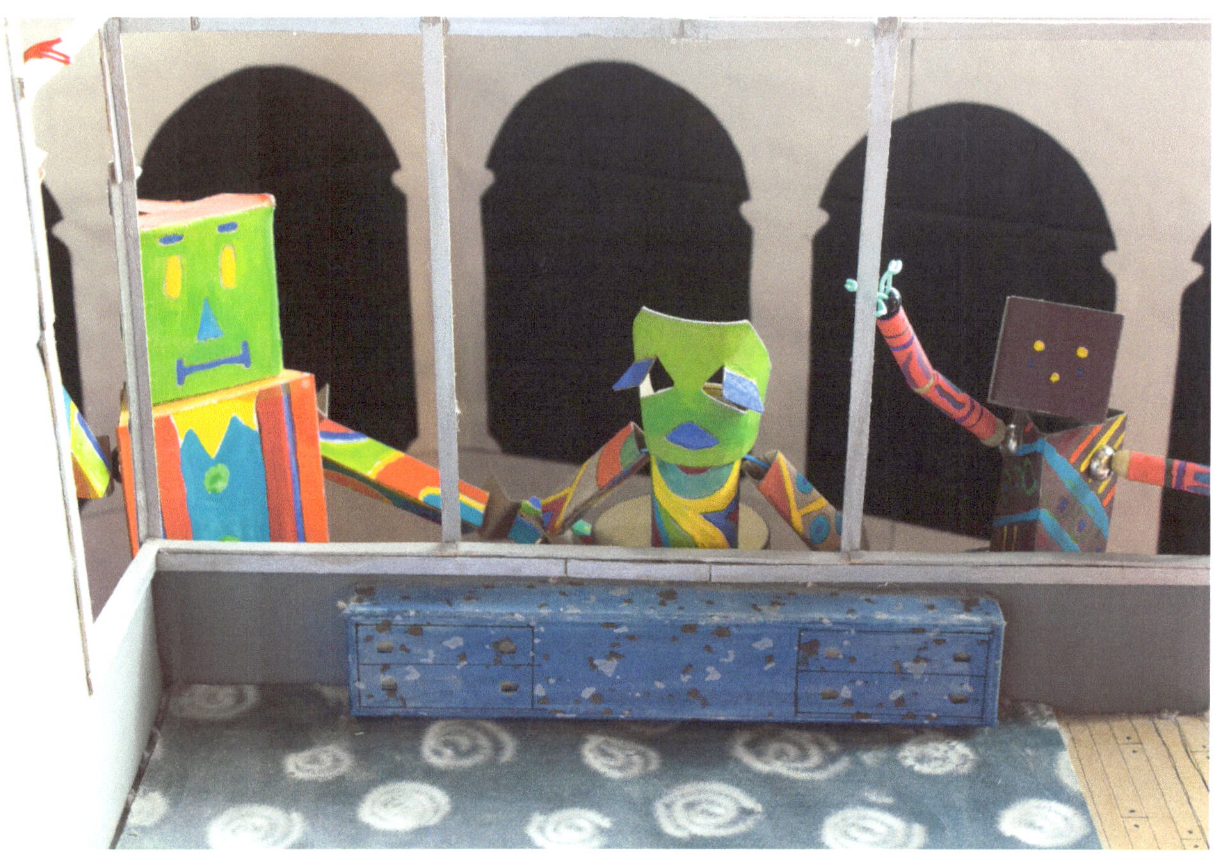

The colors are looking at you.

But wonder is not always, does not have to be innocent. We talk about wonder as if it strikes us without invitation. In fact, at this point in my middle aged life, I have made hundreds of decisions to be ready to receive it. I have cultivated some sensitivities and allowed others to fossilize and wither away. I have decided where to habitually direct the whites of my eyes. Ethics and aesthetics, always linked but never the same thing. A small paint shop fitted with carved oak shelves, where are hived all the pigments yet found, natural and unnatural, arranged for sale in minute and dizzying order… I don't know what the next world of colors looks like, or if there even is one, but I need to wake up from the 19th century. I need to leave this room.

I *can* summon at will a fantasy so intense it is practically a hallucination, of swimming in the aurora borealis. Streams of saturated color mingle in infinitely subtle combinations and separate again and they and I are flying together, the rainbow bird escaped from the empty beveled mirror. Since colors have no dimension, they are faster than thought. If I think about the speed, I realize how we are flashing along, but since it is effortless, it does not feel overwhelming. This unreality is neither material nor abstract, no form, no archetype of archetypes, no neo-Platonist nonsense. It is a sort of abyss. And I always say, I love this, I want to stay here. There are things that you see with your entire self. This infatuation attaches me to my life, and I arrange that life around it. And the abyss stares back, and the colors say, we are after all only colors. Are you sure you shouldn't be asking for something else? Even they are not sure they are that important. (What does my abyss think of Ye Olde Paint Shoppe? So far it hasn't said.)

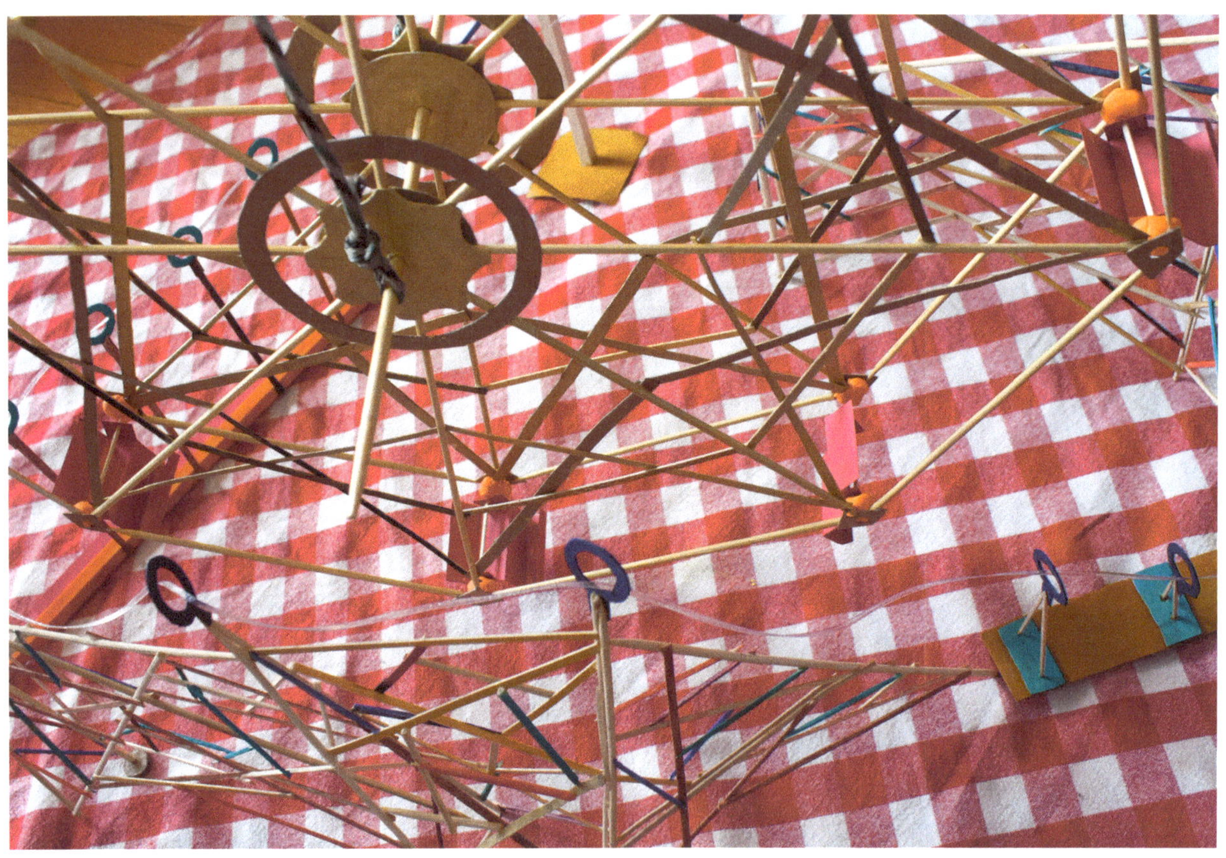

This mass delights in amusement parks—with their roller-coasters, their "twisters," their "caterpillars"—in an attitude that is pure reaction.[6]

Is this attachment adequate to the historical moment in which we find ourselves? No. No it is not. It is a necessary but insufficient condition. I do not need to hurry my own obsolescence: it is already here.

Their heads were green and their hands were blue
And they went to sea in a sieve.

But I will commit to this questionable conclusion, even as it shifts and dissolves before me like the lavender-blue flares from a driftwood fire. I consent to this seduction. I hope to be a troublesome ghost.

NOTES

White: **1.** Godwin 206-208. • **2.** Godwin 212. • **3.** Kastan 181-182. • **4.** Batchelor *Chromophobia* 9-10. • **5.** *me ni ureshi/ koi gimi no ogi/ mashiro naru* (#1123 in *Buson zenshū*, hereafter BZ). • **6.** Kenkō 28f. • **7.** Hara 11. • **8.** *fuku no tsura/ sejō no hito wo/ niramu kana* (BZ #963). • **9.** Batchelor *Chromophobia* chapter 1 passim. • **10.** Harder. • **11.** Finlay 113.

Also quoted or referenced: Roland Barthes' Empire of Signs, Lewis Carroll's Alice in Wonderland, Wilkie Collins' Woman in White, Max Eastman's "At the Aquarium," Lawrence Sterne's Tristram Shandy, Alfred Lord Tennyson's "Lady of Shallott," etc.

Yellow: **1.** Parker 33. • **2.** Davenport 84-5. • **3.** Wilcox. • **4.** Goodwin 197. • **5.** Godwin 210. • **6.** *mijikayo ya/ kane mo otosanu/ kitsune-tsuki* (BZ #555). • **7.** Pastoureau *Black* 60. • **8.** Finlay 26.

John Ford's Treasure of the Sierra Madre, James Joyce's Ulysses, China Miéville's "Polynia," Charlotte Gilmore Perkins' "Yellow Wallpaper," William Butler Yeats' "Second Coming," etc.

Red: **1.** Berlin and Kay 2. • **2.** Pastoureau *Black* 40. • **3.** Batchelor *Chromophobia* 18. • **4.** Plato 1272. • **5.** Greenfield 110-111. • **6.** Anderson 153. • **7.** Greenfield chapter 3 passim. • **8.** Higham. • **9.** *wakuraba no/ kozue ayamatsu/ ringo kana* (BZ #104). • **10.** *utsukushi ya/ nowaki no ato no/ tōgarashi* (BZ #1454). • **11.** Daley.

Charlotte Brontë's Jane Eyre, Anne Carson's Autobiography of Red, Gustave Flaubert's A Sentimental Education, Sigmund Freud's Interpretation of Dreams, etc.

Blue: **1.** *asagao ya/ ichirin fukaki/ fuchi no iro* (BZ #134). • **2.** Hardin 2. • **3.** Jones. • **4.** Goodwin 250. • **5.** Parker 107. • **6.** Finlay chapt. 8 passim. • **7.** Video of the making of this pigment is available at: *https://www.youtube.com/watch?v=JBzEAt_ynvc*.

Collins (again), Joseph Cornell's diaries, Lord Dunsany's King of Elfland's Daughter, Tennyson (again), etc.

Black: **1.** Godwin 212. • **2.** A facsimile of Werner's book is available at *https://www.c82.net/werner/#preface*. • **3.** Nijhuis. • **4.** Pastoureau *Memories* 120. • **5.** Yosa Buson *Haiku Master* 164-5. • **6.** *yugarasu/ aki no aware wo/ tsuge ni keri* (BZ #2775). • **7.** *hakubai ya/ sumi kanbashiki/ kourokan* (BZ #1225). • **8.** For analysis of the ink see: *https://brbl-dl.library.yale.edu/vufind/Record/3519597*. The Beinecke has made scans of the book's pages available online: *https://beinecke.library.yale.edu/collections/highlights/voynich-manuscript*. • **9.** Pastoureau *Black* 174. • **10.** Godwin 61. • **11.** Benjamin "Paris" 18.

Frank Cowper's "Christmas Eve on a Haunted Hulk," Edgar Allen Poe's "Masque of the Red Death," JorisKarl Huysmans' Against Nature.

Brown: **1.** Using Benjamin to discuss middle-class domestic spaces as phantasmagoria is the main project of Julia Prewitt Brown's *The Bourgeois Interior.* • **2.** Benjamin "One Way Street" 447. • **3.** McCouat. • **4.** *uguisu ya/ nani gosotsukasu/ yabu no shimo* (BZ #2413). • **5.** Goodwin 250. • **6.** Ueda 68. • **7.** Collaged together from Vaché's writings (Hale, Lent, et. al.) 209-233 passim. • **8.** *chabukuro wo/ sutsuru tokoro mo/ ochiba kana* (BZ #263). • **9.** All quoted material in this and previous paragraph is from Shakespeare's article. • **10.** Godwin 20.

Robert Browning's "Childe Roland to the Dark Tower Came."

Orange: **1.** Kircher, unnumbered page. Quoted throughout chapter. • **2.** Godwin 272-273. • **3.** Kastan 44. • **4.** Smith 29. • **5.** Greenfield, unnumbered plate. • **6.** Finlay 303, 312. • **7.** Bitler. • **8.** Kastan 134-35. • **9.** *kogitsune no/ nani ni musekemu/ kohagihara* (BZ #161). • **10.** Godwin 145. • **11.** Godwin 211, Kircher 4. • **12.** Godwin 15.

St. Augustine's City of God, William Blake's "Tyger, Tyger."

Green: **1.** Pastoureaux *Black* 142-143, diagram based on illustration. • **2.** Goodwin 253. • **3.** Goodwin 20. • **4.** Jones. • **5.** Godwin 207. • **6.** *kaya wo dete/ Nara wo tachiyuku/ wakaba kana* (BZ #563). • **7.** Philipkoski.

Anne Carson's "God's Justice," Samuel Taylor Coleridge's "Christabel," Maria Dermout's Ten Thousand Things, William Shakespeare's Much Ado About Nothing.

Purple: **1.** Kastan chapter 7 passim. • **2.** *akebono no/ murasaki no baku ya/ haru no kaze* (BZ #2416). • **3.** *yoi yoi no/ame ni oto nashi/ kakitsubata* (BZ #873). • **4.** *suwaritaru/ fune o agareba/ sumire kana* (BZ #981). • **5.** Tayag.

D. H. Lawrence's "Bavarian Gentians," John Ruskin's "On the Nature of the Gothic," Oscar Wilde's Picture of Dorian Gray.

Grey: **1.** Cohen 4. • **2.** Terrence Brown. • **3.** *mizugiwa mo/ nakute Furue no/ shigure kana* (BZ #245). • **4.** Cheeke. • **5.** Goodwin 146. • **6.** Julia Prewitt Brown 74. • **7.** *mijikayo ya/makura ni chikaki/ ginbyōbu* (BZ #756).

William Butler Yeats's Collected Poems.

Afterword: **1.** Garfield 79-80. • **2.** Quoted in Batchelor *Luminous* 39. • **3.** Batchelor *Chromophobia* 23, 27, Kastan 189. • **4.** Godwin 211; Benjamin "A Child's View" 50. • **5.** Batchelor *Luminous* 32. • **6.** Benjamin "Paris" 18.

Elizabeth Bishop's "Sonnet," Edward Lear's "Jumblies," Proust's *Swann's Way, Psilocybe cubensis.*

BIBLIOGRAPHY

Anderson, Earl R. *Folk Taxonomies in Early English.* Fairleigh Dickinson UP, 2003.

Batchelor, David. *Chromophobia.* London: Reaktion Books, 2000.

-----. *The Luminous and the Grey.* London: Reaktion Books, 2014.

Benjamin, Walter. "A Child's View of Color." *Selected Writings Volume 1,* 50-51. Marcus Bullock and Michael W. Jennings, editors. Cambridge, MA: Harvard UP, 1996.

-----. "One Way Street." *Selected Writings Volume 1* (see above), 444-487.

-----. "Paris, the Capital of the 19th Century: Exposé of 1935." *The Arcades Project* 3-13. Howard Eiland and Kevin McLaughlin, translators. Cambridge, MA: Harvard UP, 2003.

Berlin, Brent and Paul Kay. *Basic Color Terms: Their Universality and Evolution.* Stanford, CA: Center for the Study of Language and Information, 1999.

Bitler, James. "Indigo." *New Georgia Encyclopedia,* June 8, 2017.

Brown, Julia Prewitt. *The Bourgeois Interior: How the Middle Class Imagines Itself in Literature and Film.* Charlottesville, VA: University of Virginia Press, 2008.

Brown, Terrence. "Yeats and the Colours of Poetry." *The Living Stream: Essays in Memory of A. Norman Jeffares.* Warwick Gould, editor. 57-68. Cambridge: Open Book Publishers, 2015.

Buson: see Yosa Buson

Carson, Anne. *Autobiography of Red.* New York: Alfred A. Knopf, 1998.

-----. "God's Justice." *Glass, Irony and God.* New Directions, 1995.

Cheeke, Stephen. "The Wonderful and Frightening World of W. B. Yeats." [Video] Best of Bristol Lectures, University of Bristol. May 18, 2016. *https://www.youtube.com/watch?v=5LckgJgGNd0.*

Cohen, Margaret. *Profane Illumination.* Berkeley: University of California Press, 1993.

Daley, Jason. "One of the Oldest 'Crayons' Colors in Details of the Mesolithic World." Smithsonian.com, February 1, 2018.

Davenport, Guy. *Objects on a Table: Harmonious Disarray in Art and Literature.* Washington, D.C: Counterpoint, 1998.

Eastman, Max. "At the Aquarium." *https://www.bartleby.com/104/96.html.*

Garfield, Simon. *Mauve: How One Man Invented a Color that Changed the World.* New York: Norton, 2000.

Godwin, Joscylen. *Athanasius Kircher's Theatre of the World: The Life and Work of the Last Man to Search for Universal Knowledge.* Rochester, VT: Inner Traditions, 2009.

Greenfield, Amy Butler. *A Perfect Red: Empire, Espionage, and the Quest for the Color of Desire.* New York: Harper Collins, 2005.

Finlay, Victoria. *Color: A Natural History of the Palette.* New York: Random House, 2004.

Hale, Terry, Paul Lenti, Iain White, etc., translators. *Four Dada Suicides: Selected Texts of Arthur Craven, Jacques Rigault, Julien Torma and Jacques Vaché.* London: Atlas Press, 1995.

Hara, Kenya. *White.* Zurich: Lars Müller, 2009.

Harder, Jeff. "What If You Drink Bleach?" *How Stuff Works.* https://science.howstuffworks.com/science-vs-myth/what-if/what-if-drink-bleach.htm.

Hardin, C. L. "Berlin and Kay Theory." *Encyclopedia of Color Science and Technology.* Springer Science+Business Media New York, 2013.

Higham, James P. "The Red and Green Specialists: Why Human Colour Vision is So Odd." *Aeon Media Group,* February 6, 2018.

Jones, Nicola. "Do You See What I See?" *Sapiens,* February 9, 2017.

Kastan, David Scott, with Stephen Farthing. *On Color.* New Haven, CT: Yale UP, 2018.

Kenkō. *Essays in Idleness: The Tzurezuregusa of Kenkō.* Donald Keene, translator. New York: Columbia UP, 1998.

Kircher, Athanasius. *The Volcanos: Or Burning and Fire Vomiting Mountains, Famous in the World (1699).* Whitefish, Montana: Kessinger Legacy Reprints.

McCouat, Philip. "The Life and Death of Mummy Brown." *Journal of Art in Society,* www.artinsociety.com.

Mieville, China. "Polynia." *Three Moments of an Explosion.* New York: Del Ray, 2015, 5-22.

Nijhuis, Michelle. "The Book that Colored Charles Darwin's World." *New Yorker,* January 27, 2018.

Parker, Steve. *Color and Vision: The Evolution of Eyes and Perception.* Richmond Hill, ON: Firefly Books, 2016.

Pastoureau, Michel. *Black: The History of a Color.* Princeton, NJ: Princeton UP, 2008.

-----. *The Colours of Our Memories.* Janet Lloyd, translator. Cambridge, UK: Polity Press, 2012.

Philipkoski, Kristen. "This Artist Painted with Poison." *Wired,* June 12, 2003.

Plato. *Complete Works.* John M. Cooper, editor. Indianapolis: Hackett Publishing, 1997.

Shakespeare, Alex. "The Letter as Literature: Jacques Vaché." *The Battersea Review* v. 2 #6, fall 2016.

Smith, A. Mark. *From Sight to Light: The Passage from Ancient to Modern Optics.* University of Chicago Press, 2015.

Syme, Patrick. *Werner's Nomenclature of Colours Adapted to Zoology, Botany, Chemistry, Mineralogy, Anatomy, and the Arts.* London: Natural History Museum of London, 2018.

Tayag, Yasmin. "Sir William Henry Perkin Accidentally Kickstarted a Chemical Disaster." *Inverse,* March 12, 2018.

Ueda, Makoto. *The Path of Flowering Thorn: The Life and Poetry of Yosa Buson.* Stanford, CA: Stanford University Press, 1998.

Wilcox, Christie. "Meet the Trumpapillar: The Venomous Caterpillar that Perfectly Mimics the Donald's Hair." *Discover Magazine,* October 6, 2016.

Yosa Buson. *Buson zenshū.* Morita Ran and Ogata Tsutomu, editors. Tokyo: Kodansha, 1992.

Yosa Buson. *Haiku Master Buson.* Yuki Sawa and Edith Shiffert, translators. Union City, CA: Heian International, 1978

www.ingramcontent.com/pod-product-compliance
Lightning Source LLC
LaVergne TN
LVHW070213110826
845147LV00003B/567

* 9 7 8 0 9 8 2 5 6 4 7 2 1 *